D1004590

be.attitudes

Kathy A. Weckwerth

Kathy A. Weckwerth

be.attitudes

... be.inspired ... be.motivated ... be.blessed

A Women's 10 week Bible Study

Shaping Your Heart With Godly Attitudes From Matthew 5

be.attitudes
by Kathy A. Weckwerth

Published by Creative Days, Inc.
P.O. Box 73
Benson, Minnesota 56215

Cover Design: Peter Grossman
Compiled by: Marea Anderson
Editor: Susan C. Snow

Visit the author's website at www.KathyWeckwerth.com
Visit the author's ministry website at www.bestlifeministries.com

ISBN: 978-1-312-21716-4

To my amazing parents, who spent their everyday lives teaching us all about having a Godly attitude.
I am forever ... blessed.

be.attitudes

Shaping Your Heart With Godly Attitudes From Matthew 5

Introduction ~ Having Christ-like Attitudes in Your Everyday Life ... 1

Blessed Are the Poor in Spirit ... 9

Blessed Are Those Who Mourn ... 21

Blessed Are the Meek ... 33

Blessed Are Those Who Hunger and Thirst After Righteousness ... 47

Blessed Are the Merciful ... 59

Blessed Are the Pure in Heart ... 75

Blessed Are the Peacemakers ... 91

Blessed Are Those Who Are Persecuted ... 103

Conclusion ~ Implementing Godly Attitudes ... 117

be.attitudes

Introduction

be.attitudes

"A Christian is never in a state of completion but always in the process of becoming."

Martin Luther

Be. Focused Be. Encouraged Be. Your Best

The Beatitudes: *Shaping your heart with Godly attitudes*

I ran to pick up the phone and I answered with a breathless, "Hello?"

My oldest daughter was in tears. "Mom, I can't take it anymore!" she exclaimed exasperated.

"What's happening?" I asked.

"It's this neighborhood. No one understands what it's like to live here. I'm a mom with two little boys, two rat terrier dogs, three lizards, two cats, a bunch of baby robins in a birds' nest above the door, and a husband with a lot of golf clubs. Everyone else who lives here is older, single, and doesn't even have a goldfish."

"I know, I know," I tried to console her.

"Now, one of the neighbors has called to report me to the townhouse association, and the association manager is telling me that along with every tricycle, bicycle, box of pampers, bag of cat chow, and my gas grill, I will now have to store my car and my garbage cans inside my one car garage. I can't take it! I hate this place. These people don't get it. I hate my neighborhood." She let out a sob and finished "Why would someone do that? I am so mad. I am so angry. I know I have a bad attitude, but I refuse to ever speak to any of them again. I don't want to live in this neighborhood."

> In our everyday lives, attitude is everything.
>
> 

After a half hour of listening and trying to bring comfort, I told my daughter that short of picking up everything she owns and moving out of the neighborhood with her small San Diego Zoo in tow, she had to grasp a *better attitude* towards the association, the neighbors, and the entire neighborhood.

In our everyday lives, *attitude is everything*. We hear it. We know it. We get it. But we are continually faced with a world that spins and twirls in orbit, while we are thrust out onto the concrete each day, to once again face one tough situation and circumstance after another.

There will be episodes in my life that require my attention, my reaction, and my response. Everyday circumstances will occur that elicit my reactions and my *attitudes*. Possible reactions will buzz around in my head. Some reactions will be delivered with an attitude that stings and makes life difficult and problematic. Other reactions will be flowing with sweet honey that makes life meaningful and joy-filled ... happy and *blessed*.

Attitudes are a funny thing. They are what makes us or breaks us. More often than not, I am broken and crushed at the core of my being by something that has happened or someone who has hurt me. My attitude trickles right out of my mouth through bitter words, my emotions are perpetuated as the driving force behind that old thing known as *attitude*. I become angry, bitter, resentful, and eventually obnoxious. Everything is drawn to the surface because Jesus tells us in Luke 6:45b, "*Out of the overflow of the heart the mouth speaks.*" That attitude, that I'm not controlling myself because my emotions have the best of me, is now surfacing and adding more trouble, strife, and conflict to my life. What can I do? What can you do when this describes *your* life?

In Matthew chapter 5, Jesus begins to give us the answers that we need to help us on our journey, teaching us how to develop attitudes that will not break us, but will build into us, create Christ-like-characteristics, and ultimately make us better. These are the attitudes of the heart. These are the attitudes that we, as Christ-followers, must grasp, embrace, and walk out to be the best version of who we can be. The beatitudes that Jesus teaches in Matthew are eight characteristics, eight attitudes for life ... *your life ... a better life.*

The word *beatitude* comes from the Latin word for happy, *beatitudo*, which means "blessedness." In His sermon, Jesus was saying "happy and blessed" are those who possess these inward attributes and attitudes. We need to be aware that each current themed "blessedness" delivered by Jesus, also promises a future reward.

Matthew reports to us in chapter 4 that in order to reach a wider audience, Jesus moved from Nazareth to the city of Capernaum, on the shores of the Sea of Galilee, and delivers His first and longest message that we know of, ever recorded in the life of Jesus.

Before we spread our blanket on the soft grassy earth and imagine sitting back to listen to the words of this Jesus that we've heard so much about, we must rewind the clock and look back in time at what the prophet Isaiah predicted would happen.

 **Look Up Isaiah 61:1**

"The Spirit of the Sovereign Lord is on me, because the Lord has anointed me to preach good news to the poor. He has sent me to bind up the brokenhearted, to proclaim freedom for the captives and release from darkness for the prisoners."

The four things that Isaiah tells us that the Messiah is going to do for mankind is listed in this prophetic verse: 1) Preach good news to the poor 2) Bind up the brokenhearted 3) Proclaim freedom for the captives 4) Release prisoners from darkness.

 **Look Up: Isaiah 52:7**

"How beautiful on the mountains are the feet of those who bring good news."

Who is bringing the good news? The Lord's anointed, the Messiah. The word Christ comes from the Greek word *khristos,* from a little verb *krio,* which meant "to anoint."

 **Look Up: Matthew 4:17**

"From that time on, Jesus began to preach, 'Repent, the kingdom of heaven has come near.'"

Jesus calls for people to repent, to change their lives, to ask for forgiveness and make over their hearts. Change your attitudes. Be Christ-like.

 **Look Up: Matthew 4:23-24**

"Jesus went through Galilee, teaching in their synagogues, proclaiming the good news. News about Him spreads all over Syria. And people brought to Him all who were ill with various diseases, those sufferings severe pain,

the demon-possessed, those having seizures and the paralyzed, and He healed them."

The crowds are gathering looking for the good news. What's the good news? The Kingdom of God is at hand. The Messiah has come. He is here to save the people from their sins. He's here, right here, in our own neighborhood.

The feet of Jesus are now standing on the mountainside. The crowds are coming forth. They've heard of the Messiah's message, His healing, His miracles, His preaching the good news.

Look Up: Matthew 5:1-2

"When Jesus saw his ministry drawing huge crowds, he climbed a hillside. Those who were apprenticed to him, the committed, climbed with him. Arriving at a quiet place, he sat down and taught his climbing companions."

Jesus begins his sermon, known as The Sermon on the Mount, and starts with what we know as the *beatitudes* by saying, *"Blessed."* A God filled with love for His people, sends His Son for us, to dwell and live here on earth, giving us the directions, the steps, and the pieces to make our lives better by saying "live like this." He gives us these attitudes to soak up and embrace, so that we can know the kind of everyday life we can live, our very best version of who we are meant to be. Promises that begin with *"Blessed."*

Being blessed by God means that we will listen to His direction, embrace His attitudes towards how to walk out our everyday life, and feel contentment for abiding by His design. We will experience hope and joy, independent of our outward circumstances. Romans 12:1 states, *"So here's what I want you to do, God helping you: Take your everyday, ordinary life, your sleeping, eating, going to work, and walking around life-and place it before God as an offering" (MSG).*

What will the offering of our lives look like to God? Will we be humble, self-sacrificing, meek, seeking God with an expectant hope, merciful, pure in heart and totally dependent on God, peace-making and Christ-like, sharing the gospel? The beatitudes are the *attitudes of the heart, mind, and spirit*, all given to us in simplistic steps. They are the attitudes to live by.

Our attitudes must remain concurrent with God's Word. To be blessed by having an utter dependency on God alone, means that we will experience joy and blessing above our outward experiences.

The good news has arrived on the mountain that sunny, warm day. The grass is soft and inviting as we spread our blanket out and prepare to hear the most compelling eight attitudes of the soul that we will ever hear. Jesus will share the "*be attitudes*" (beatitudes) and teach us how to live each and every moment that we walk this earth.

As we look around us now, amidst the crowd, we recognize the faces of our neighbors and begin to grasp what's happening on this warm afternoon. The Messiah has come. The good news is delivered. Salvation is ours. This is the place you want to live. This is the place your children want to live. This is the neighborhood of Christ. This is the truth from the lips of the Savior. Live and dwell inside the Word. "*The Word became flesh and blood and moved into the neighborhood*." John 1:14 *(MSG).*

Questions:

1. How often do you find that your emotions have taken over your attitude?

2. Have you ever been affected by someone else's attitude?

3. Are you routinely aware of what attitudes you are embracing?

4. What ungodly attitude are you wrestling with today?

 **Look up:**

1. **Hebrews 12:3**
2. **Psalm 119:5**
3. **Philippians 1:6**
4. **II Corinthians 5:17**
5. **Romans 12:1**
6. **Philippians 2:5-11**

 **Songs:**

Hymn - *"Blessed Assurance"*

Contemporary - *"One Thing Remains" (Johnson, Gifford, Riddle)*

Closing Prayer:

Dear Jesus, please help me
to leave my emotions
at Your feet.

Please help me to realize
that my attitude
can make a difference in those
around me
and how they're reacting
and responding
to difficult
and challenging
circumstances.

Today, I commit to you
that I will remain peace-filled
and seek You for truth,
wisdom, and direction
in my everyday walk,
and that I will allow
Your attitudes to permeate
my heart, mind, and spirit.
In Jesus' Name, *Amen*.

CHAPTER 1

Poor In Spirit

"Humility does not mean thinking less of yourself than of other people, nor does it mean having a low opinion of your own gifts. It means freedom from thinking about yourself at all."

Archbishop William Temple

Be. Humble   Be. God-Reliant   Be. Blessed

The Buzz Last week we learned that attitude is everything. In Matthew 5, Jesus delivers the attitudes that need to shape our hearts so we can live a life that is truly blessed.

Matthew 5:3 *"Blessed are the poor in spirit, for theirs is the Kingdom of Heaven."*

I can never forget, nor would I ever want to forget that dark and stormy night, where God reminded me of the true meaning of the word ... *humility.*

At the time, I was serving as a worship director in a local church when a neighboring congregation called me to ask if I would bring our worship team and settle in for a month long series of consulting them to develop a worship arts ministry.

Electric guitars, amps, and microphones, were dragged through the hallways of the church that Sunday evening. We began to set up everything and prepared for a much anticipated evening of worship.

One by one, people quietly entered, uncertain, unsure, but ready for whatever would take place. A storm had settled into the cool summer evening, and as people entered the sanctuary, bright bolts of lightning flashed, again and again.

Each time the loud cracks of thunder rumbled, we were reminded of God's power and holiness that seemed to demand a reverent spirit. A thought crossed my mind as I looked up at the big stained glass windows and shuddered with a reminder that He is God and we are not.

I lined up our team and did a quick sound check. The excitement in the air was reminiscent of electric static, as we welcomed a group of about forty-five people. Suddenly, as we began to sing, lightening struck and rendered us inoperable. No power. With no power came no lights, no electric amps, no electric guitars, no microphones for singers ... nothing. The leftover daylight created dark shadows in the room.

I did the only thing I know how to do when panic-stricken and in shock. I asked everyone to bow their heads and pray. People were in a reverent awe over the atmosphere. It was not what we wanted. It was not how we planned it. It was God's plan, and the evening began to unfold.

The music was hard to read in the early evening storm hours, but fortunately, I knew a couple songs by heart and as I played I quietly prayed and said to God, "Why are you doing this? They wanted to praise You. They wanted to offer up worship. They invited us here to show them how to do this. We know how. Aren't you going to let us show them what we know?" I questioned Him.

I have to admit to you that up until this moment, I didn't believe that any of us were prideful, but as soon as God rendered us inoperable, I realized that pride had flittered its way, like a small moth, into the back doors and small windows of our hearts.

I felt the Spirit of God whisper to me, "They want to know how to worship. They want to understand the heart of true worship. It's not at all about what you can do, Kathy, *it's about all that I can do*."

Humbled ... waiting ... we anticipated what God would do next. No, we didn't anticipate ... we hungered for God. We waited on God. We were quiet. I played quietly, and someone placed a candle on the piano for me. I began to lead simple choruses. I realized that in the darkness of that room, an awe of reverence had taken over our great enthusiasm to "*show them how it's done*."

Simply ... quietly ... reverently bowed before a Mighty God ... we sang. The beautiful stained glass windows shone in brilliant subtle hues of blues and browns as electric lightning bolts raced through the sky and illuminated the glorious essence of Christ hanging on the cross.

We had no power. No control. We were humbled. We were reverent. We were again reminded that nothing that we do is glorious. Nothing we create, sing, say, or play can ever come close to the amazing power of the glorious God that we worship.

> We cannot operate or even fathom trying to be Christ like, if we do not begin each day by humbling ourselves before God and then before others.

After many moments singing in the darkness, I humbled myself before a God that deserved only my best. Pride had snuck in without me even recognizing it, and into the simplest form of worship. Just as I closed my eyes to ask for forgiveness, a slap of thunder permeated the room and the lights were back on again. God was in control. I had nothing to offer, knew nothing except this one thing ... God was God and I was not. He was the one worthy of honor, attention, and praise.

The attitude of humility is invaluable. We cannot operate or even fathom trying to be Christ-like, if we do not begin each day by humbling ourselves before God and then before others.

Look Up: 1 Peter 5:5

"Likewise, you who are younger, be subject to the elders. Clothe yourselves, all of you, with humility toward one another, for God opposes the proud but gives grace to the humble."

In the moments when we are self-reliant and certain that *we* can do it, that *we* are in control, that *our* plan is best, then we are rendered inoperable for doing what *God* needs us to do.

"To be poor in spirit is not to lack courage but to acknowledge spiritual bankruptcy. It confesses one's unworthiness before God and utter dependence on Him," states Carson, in the *Expositor's Bible Commentary.*

In order for us to begin to live a life that is blessed through humility, we must learn to humble ourselves. This means to cast off not only those self-reliant attitudes, but the selfish motivations that take over our minds and hearts.

One of my favorite women's authors from long ago, Catherine Marshall, said this about humility, *"Once we recognize our need for Jesus, then the building of our faith begins. It is a daily, moment-by-moment life of absolute dependence upon Him for everything."*

So often in today's society, we are living with the *fast* mentality. We become overly anxious when we have to wait for our internet connection, wait on the phone or in a line at a store, or wait for our fast food order. Waiting is no longer an option. What does that have to do with humility? We are self-focused. We are self-reliant. We think about ourselves first, foremost, and continually! Our attitudes must change, reformat, reboot, and recycle to once again place God first and others next. We've forgotten that people are important and now a lack of reverence for the Almighty God has permeated the place where our heart resides.

Webster's Dictionary states that *humility* means, "*The quality of being modest or respectful*," and the synonyms for this word are as follows: "self-effacement (*avoid drawing attention to yourself*), unpretentiousness (*not putting on a false or showy display of importance*), humbleness, modesty."

In order to live out an attitude of being "poor in spirit," we must begin to be humble. We must wear humility around our shoulders like a warm woolen sweater on a cold stormy night.

Scripture tells us over and over that in order to be Christ-like, we must be and remain humble in spirit.

 **Look Up: Isaiah 66:1-2**

"This is what the Lord says: 'Heaven is my throne, and the earth is my footstool. Where is the house you will build for me? Where will my resting place be? ... This is the one I esteem: he who is ***humble*** *and contrite in spirit, and trembles at my word.'"*

As Jesus begins with the simple words, "Blessed are the poor in spirit, for theirs is the kingdom of Heaven," we look at that word poor. *Poor* is taken from an Aramaic *'ányâ* or from Hebrew *'anî*, meaning "*bent down, afflicted, or miserable*."

Jesus begins this eight-step process of being blessed, happy, and content, by delivering a promise that the kingdom of Heaven belongs only to those who recognize their poverty of spirit, and become humble.

We begin by looking at the words of the prophet Isaiah about his commission.

 **Look Up: Isaiah 6:1-9**

Isaiah says that he "*... saw the Lord seated on a throne, high and exalted ... above Him there were seraphs ... and they were calling to one another, 'Holy, Holy, Holy is the Lord Almighty ... the whole earth is full of His glory.'*" Then Isaiah cries out in verse 5, *"Woe to me! ... I am ruined! For I am a man of unclean lips and my eyes have seen the King, the Lord Almighty."*

When God is praised and exalted above all, above our own self-centeredness and ourselves, we are aware of our own sinful nature and our need of God's mercy and forgiveness.

Being "poor in spirit" does not mean that we have a down and out or a poor-me mentality. It means that we are humble before God and focused on others first and foremost. It means that we take a position of reverence before God and before others.

Scripture shows us many examples through Biblical characters.

 **Look Up:**

1. **I Kings 21:29 (Ahab)**

2. **Philippians 3:7-8, I Timothy 1:15 (Paul)**

3. **Job 42:5-6 (Job)**

4. **Genesis 18:27 (Abraham)**

5. **Genesis 32:10 (Jacob)**

6. **John 1:27, 3:30 (John the Baptist)**

I love this quote by Shirley Dobson, wife of the James Dobson, beloved founder of Focus on the Family, "*Repentance removes old sins and wrong attitudes, and it opens the way for the Holy Spirit to restore our spiritual health.*"

How can we do this? How can we develop a healthy attitude of humility? Here are some steps that I believe will get us on the right pathway.

STEP ONE: *Recognize* that we are unworthy of God's goodness and forgiveness and confess our sins

James 5:16, "Therefore, confess your sins to each other, and pray for each other so that you may be healed. The prayer of a righteous man is powerful and effective."

I John 1:9, "If we confess our sins, He is faithful and just to forgive us our sins and to cleanse us from all unrighteousness."

II Chronicles 7:14, "If my people who are called by My name, will *humble* themselves and pray and seek My face and turn from their wicked ways, then I will hear from Heaven and I will forgive their sin and heal their land."

Romans 3:23, "For all have sinned and come short of the glory of God."

STEP TWO: *Eliminate* all pride, arrogance, and self reliance

Isaiah 53:5, "... by His stripes we are healed."

I Peter 2:24-25, "Who Himself bore our sins in His own body on the tree, that we, having died to sins, might live for righteousness-by whose stripes you were healed. For you were like sheep going astray, but have now returned to the Shepherd and Overseer of your souls" *(NKJV).*

Psalm 55:19, "God will give ear and humble them, he who is enthroned from of old, Selah because they do not change and do not fear God."

Hebrews 8:12, "I will be merciful to their unrighteousness, and their sins and their lawless deeds I will remember no more."

STEP THREE: *Bow* before God and submit to His will

Psalm 25:9, "He leads the humble in what is right, and teaches the humble His way."

I Peter 5:5, "Likewise, you who are younger, be subject to the elders. Clothe yourselves, all of you, with humility toward one another, for 'God opposes the proud but gives grace to the humble.'"

Psalm 95:6, "Come let us worship and bow down, let us kneel before the Lord our maker."

James 4:10, "When you bow down before the Lord and admit your dependence on Him, He will lift you up and give you honor."

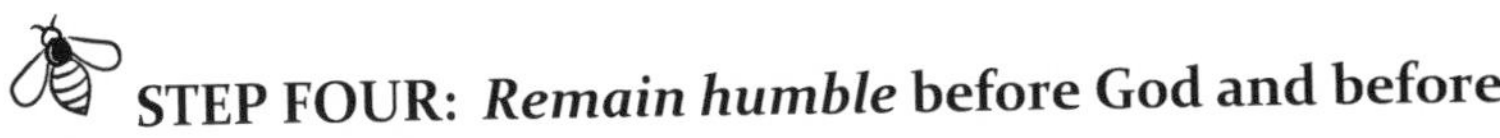

STEP FOUR: ***Remain humble*** **before God and before others**

Zechariah 9:9, "Rejoice greatly, O daughter of Zion! Shout aloud, O daughter of Jerusalem! Behold, your king is coming to you; righteous and having salvation is he, humble and mounted on a donkey, on a colt, the foal of a donkey."

Mark 10:45, "For even the Son of Man came not to be served but to serve, and to give his life as a ransom for many."

Philippians 2:5-8, "Have this mind among yourselves, which is yours in Christ Jesus, who, though He was in the form of God, did not count equality with God a thing to be grasped, but emptied Himself, by taking the form of a servant, being born in the likeness of men. And being found in human form, He humbled himself by becoming obedient to the point of death, even death on a cross."

Deuteronomy 8:2-3, "And you shall remember the whole way that the Lord your God has led you these forty years in the wilderness, that He might humble you, testing you to know what was in your heart, whether you would keep His commandments or not. And He humbled you and let you hunger and fed you with manna, which you did not know, nor did your fathers know, that He might make you know that man does not live by bread alone, but man lives by every word that comes from the mouth of the Lord."

As Christ followers, as long as we're alive, each one of us will continue to grow in knowledge, until the Lord calls us to be with Him. Each one of us will continually struggle with being submissive to God, obedient to confess our sins, and willing to remain humble. The sooner we accept that we don't know everything, and we can grow and learn daily, the sooner God can build into us greater, richer knowledge that He has in store for us, and then we will become better followers of Him. We will be happy. We will be content. We will be blessed.

God wants us to be free from allowing our emotions to have control over our every attitude and move we make. Instead of our attitudes controlling us, He's calling us to control our attitudes. We must be poor in spirit before we can become rich in blessings.

Questions:

1. When do you struggle with prideful feelings? For example: Do you feel like you are always right?

2. Share a time you found yourself putting the needs and desires of those around you first.

3. Are you regularly seeking God and confessing sin? Or do you consider yourself someone who is self-reliant and blameless?

4. What will you do today to pursue a humble attitude about yourself and your importance, balancing it out with what God says in scripture?

Look Up:

1. **Isaiah 57:15**
2. **Isaiah 66:2**
3. **Jeremiah 10:23**
4. **I Corinthians 3:18**

Songs:

Hymn - *"Holy, Holy, Holy"*

Contemporary - *"How Great Is Our God" (Tomlin)*

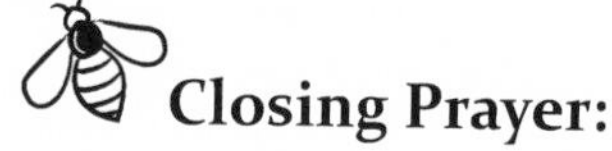

Closing Prayer:

Dear Jesus, forgive me for my sins.
Forgive me for continually falling short of Your glory.
Forgive me for the times that I put myself first
and am self-reliant, self-focused, and self-centered.

Today, I ask that You would
give me the ability to be Christ-like.
I humble myself before You,
admitting that You are the one and only God
and I present myself to You as a living sacrifice.
Use me to bless others and be the hands and feet of Christ.
In Jesus' Name, *Amen.*

CHAPTER 2

Those Who Mourn 

"What joy that the Bible tells us the great comfort that the best is yet to be. Our outlook goes beyond this world."

Corrie Ten Boom

Be. Authentic Be. Comforted Be. Blessed

The Buzz: Last week we learned that "the poor in spirit" means those who are humble before God. We are blessed when we have an attitude of humility.

Matthew 5:4 *"Blessed are those who mourn, for they will be comforted."*

When I was a little girl of three and four, my daddy would call my siblings, my mother, and me to the car when it was time to leave for Sunday morning church services.

I knew my spot. It never failed that I would sit directly in the middle of my parents in the front seat. It never dawned on me that I would be anywhere except next to my daddy. It wasn't good enough that I was seat belted in next to him, but I had to be so close to him that I would crowd him. It felt safe there. It was comforting. It was where I wanted to be, right next to Dad.

My father was a kind and patient soul. He would say to me, "Kathleen, honey, you can't be quite so close because Daddy needs to be able to drive the car." I'd scoot over just a smidgen as he would start up the old Chevy and lead the way to our little blue church.

As the years passed and I went through grade school, my father was always there providing a sense of security. I remember one cool summer evening where we had come home one day early from vacation. My dad sensed that we were to leave immediately, and I still remember the feeling of disappointment my siblings and I felt as we headed for home.

Around 1:00 a.m. in the morning, I heard my father whispering loudly. I threw my covers off and crept quietly to my bedroom door peering down the hall. I watched my father, gun in tow, as he slithered as if he was out on the battlefield, avoiding grenades and enemy tactics, making his way quietly down the hallway. My mother crossed the hallway and told me to go into my room and hide underneath the bed. I watched as my sister followed directions carefully, and my brother pushed past me hurrying to hide with her.

I needed to see what would happen to Dad. I could not hide. I snuck out and followed him without him knowing. A dark sedan was parked in our driveway with the lights on and the car running. Because we lived on a dead-end road, I knew there was trouble. I looked past my daddy's shoulder and saw a man sitting in the front seat putting out a cigarette. He got out of the car, headed to the front door, and grasped the knob. My father flicked the outside light on, which scared the man, and he ran to his car and tore out of the driveway. My father put his gun down, swept me up in one big swoop and carried me to the phone where he calmly dialed the police to make a description. Dad knew that the man meant no good, and probably had been watching our house for days.

I remember another day that as a teenager, I ran all the way home from lunch, sobbing as I ran. A young boy in my class had vandalized my locker and all of my possessions, marking them up with a big "Jesus Saves" to try to embarrass me. Everything was ruined and I felt the shunning and whispers of my classmates. My heart grieved not just for my possessions, but also for why I would have to be harassed for following Jesus.

My daddy, a college professor, came home for lunch that day, and wondered why I was sobbing in my room. He came in and sat at the end of the bed and asked, "Kathleen, what's wrong?"

As I told him everything that had taken place that morning, he smiled so big and hugged me. He said, "Let's look at this whole thing from a different perspective. Isn't it great that he marked up your books and locker with truth? What a great thing to know that you are proudly displaying the message of Christ everyday! Jesus does save."

I looked at him and thought he's right! Dad offered me a cold sandwich and glass of milk (*my mother worked during the day and was not home at lunchtime*) and walked me out to the car, gently talking to me and offering a ride back to school.

The years continued to go by and I think of how many times I looked to my father for wisdom, guidance, and comfort. As I grew into a young married mom of three girls, working for churches, just living life, there was always a situation where I needed my dad.

The hardest of times came for me during a devastating divorce. I called my father, knowing how he felt about divorce, to tell him about my spouse's double life. I had never experienced such grief and could not find my way out of the fog. My father brought comfort and these words to my aid, as he said, "I am so very, very sorry. Your mom and I support you 1000% and we will be there in about ... seven hours." My parents lived nine hours away.

A few weeks later, my father knew that I was experiencing the deepest level of sadness, anger, and grief I'd ever known. Now, no longer a child but a grown mother of three, I listened as he once again sat at the end of my bed and wept bitterly saying that he should have come and got me the first week I was married, when I called him and said that the person I thought I married was not really who I married. My father wept.

Several years ago, I sat at the end of my father's bed while he prepared himself for leaving this old world. He looked at me, amid tubes and the beeps of the hospital machines, smiled and said, "Kathleen, you know the greatest thing I ever did while I was here?"

"No, Daddy, what was it?" I asked, thinking he'd talk about his invention of a grenade launcher for Honeywell to assist our soldiers in the Vietnam War, or twenty-five plus years of teaching students, or the church plants he'd been a part of, but instead my father said the words I will never forget.

He said, "I always believed that I was put on this earth to be a dad. Your dad. Your brother's dad. Your sister's dad. I was here to just be a dad."

In the moments of wondering if there was any way that someone else could understand my grief, I grew up knowing and feeling that comfort, that sense of safety, inside the arms of my earthly father. But how much greater is the love for us that our Heavenly Father has to offer?

The attitude of mourning is understandable. In order to be Christ-like, we must begin by being honest before God and allow Him to comfort us.

> In order to be Christ-like, we must begin by being honest before God.
>
> 

Whether we are mourning about what we have done, or what's happening in our lives because of our choices, because of others' choices, or because we live in a sin-filled, fallen world, we must mourn. We need to mourn. Mourning allows us to draw close to the side of our Heavenly Father.

 **Look Up: Psalm 119:136**

"Tears stream down from my eyes, because they do not keep Your law."

 **Look Up: Psalm 30:5b**

"Weeping may last through the night, but joy comes with the morning."

Very often in life, I have watched people try to minimize the pain of others. I've questioned why people do this, and I believe it stems from these three things:

1. They don't know how to bring comfort.
2. They don't want to deal with the person and their problem.
3. They hold back because no one helps them, so they don't want to help others.

Webster's dictionary defines the word *mourn* as *"to feel and show sadness because something has been lost or no longer exists."*

When Jesus is sitting amongst His disciples and the crowd, why would He tell them that blessed (*happy*) is the person who mourns, when the words are totally opposite?

John R. W. Stott states, *"No doubt the crowds were already getting uneasy at His unconventional philosophy of life, for He was saying things which on the surface seemed absurd. Especially so to the original audience, which consisted of disgruntled Jews living in Roman occupied Palestine, looking for a Messiah who would sweep the Romans out of the land and establish a strong kingdom, ruling with 'Blessed are they that mourn; for they shall be comforted.'" (Matthew 5:4).*

"Yet, Jesus is stating to His disciples and the crowds ... it's okay to mourn. 'It's beautiful for Me to see you grieve over your sins and I am happy to be next to you in your sadness. My blessing will be that you will be comforted, for I will bring you comfort.'"

Mourning means to feel sad and blessed means to feel happy. Christ is saying ... happy is the person who feels sad, who allows themselves to mourn, because they will be comforted. Who will comfort the mourning? God will comfort us. Some of what Jesus is saying is connected to our attitude from the first beatitude, *humility*. When we have humility, we go to God with a repentant heart that says, "I'm so sorry ... I'm grieving and mourning the fact that I have disobeyed You and gone against Your ways."

 **Look Up: Matthew 4:17**

"From that time on Jesus began to preach, 'Repent, for the kingdom of heaven has come near.'"

 **Look Up: I John 2:2**

"He is the propitiation for our sins, and not for ours only but also for the sins of the whole world."

 **Look Up: I John 1:9**

"If we confess our sins, He is faithful and just to forgive us our sins and cleanse us from all unrighteousness."

I believe the other part of this beatitude is Jesus reminding us that there is no one, no one person on earth, who will ever totally understand or comprehend what it means to suffer as greatly as He did when He died on the cross for our sins.

 **Look Up: Ephesians 3:18-19**

"*We will never find the outermost limits of Your love for us. Your love is immeasurable, inexhaustible, inescapable, irrepressible, insatiable, and irrational. O Lord, my deepest desire is to know Your love through personal experience and in my limited capacity, be filled from Your unlimited resources*" (*NIV Worship Bible*).

Jesus tells the crowds blessed are you when you mourn. The Latin word for ***to mourn*** is *lugeo* and is defined as "to *mourn, be in mourning, grieve, to lament, bewail.*"

If we are to take on the attitude of mourning, that means we will be authentic, honest, and God-serving, not self-serving. We will humbly confess our sins before Him, and in times of need, we will go to Him for comfort, for assurance, and safety.

Hannah, Job, David, and Jesus, along with many other Biblical characters went before the Lord in mourning.

 **Look Up:**

1. **I Samuel 1:11-15 (Hannah)**
2. **Job 3:1-10, 5:11 (Job)**
3. **Psalm 56:8 (David)**
4. **John 11:14-37 (Jesus)**

Dean H. Harvey states, "*The cross is a one time, visual representation of God's grief over sin.*"

An attitude of mourning means that we allow God to bring comfort. We will have trouble because we live on planet Earth. But when we accept our humanness and go before the One who can bring comfort, we will be comforted. Here are some steps that will help you to understand how to mourn and release your sin and hurts to God.

STEP ONE: *Be. authentic* by going before God and wholeheartedly seek His forgiveness and direction

Ephesians 4:22, "You were taught, with regard to your former way of life, to put off your old self, which is being corrupted by its deceitful desires ..."

Romans 6:6, "For we know that our old self was crucified with him so that the body ruled by sin might be done away with, that we should no longer be slaves to sin."

Psalm 147:3 & 5, "He heals the heartbroken and bandages their wounds ... Our Lord is great, with limitless strength."

STEP TWO: *Be. honest* by telling God everything that's in your heart

I Chronicles 16:11-12a, "Look to the Lord and His strength; seek His face always. Remember the wonders He has done ..."

I Peter 2:24-25, "Who Himself bore our sins in His own body on the tree, that we, having died to sins, might live for righteousness by whose stripes you were healed. For you were like sheep going astray, but have now returned to the Shepherd and Overseer of your souls."

Psalm 55:19, "God will give ear and humble them,
he who is enthroned from of old, Selah because they do

not change and do not fear God."

STEP THREE: *Be. hope-filled* that God will hear your hurts and meet your needs

Psalm 62:5, "Yes, my soul, find rest in God: my hope comes from Him."

Psalm 147:11, "The Lord delights in those who fear Him who put their hope in His unfailing love."

Psalm 130:5, "I wait for You, Lord, my soul waits and in Your word I put my hope."

STEP FOUR: *Be. encouraging* to others when they are experiencing grief

Romans 12:15, "Rejoice with those who rejoice; mourn with those who mourn."

Romans 15:13, "May the God of hope fill you with all joy and peace as you trust in him, so that you may overflow with hope by the power of the Holy Spirit."

Galatians 6:14, "May I never boast except in the cross of our Lord Jesus Christ, through which the world has been crucified to me, and I to the world."

Blessed are those who mourn. Blessed are those who humble themselves before God, pour out their hearts and souls, and mourn for their sins. Blessed are those who seek God when they hurt and when they need help. Blessed are those who snuggle up next to their Heavenly Daddy, feel comfort and sense safety in the arms of God their Father.

Questions:

1. Do you go directly to God when you are experiencing sorrow and grief or try to deal with it yourself?

2. Do you believe that God can and will provide comfort for you when you are at a deep level of hurting?

3. What do you do to help those around you who are hurting and experiencing grief?

4. What are some ways that help you walk through grief?

Look Up:

1. **Psalm 23:4**
2. **Psalm 28:6-7**
3. **Isaiah 57:15**
4. **Romans 8:26-28**

Songs:

Hymn - *"In the Garden"*

Contemporary -"*Wonderful, Merciful Savior" (Rodger & Wyse)*

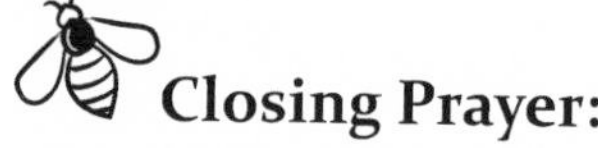

Dear Jesus, help me
to be drawn to true confession
before Your throne.
Help me to humble myself
and ask for Your help
and comfort in my times of sorrow.

Provide the true comfort
that comes only from Your Spirit.
Help me to be more like You
and to comfort those
around me who are hurting.
In Jesus' Name, *Amen.*

CHAPTER 3

Those Who Are Meek 

"The right attitude can't make you something you're not, but it can enhance everything you have and all that you are."

John Maxwell

Be. Gentle Be. Self-Controlled Be. Blessed

The Buzz: Last week we learned that "those who mourn" means that we are sorry for our sins. God will comfort us in our sadness and forgive us when we have an attitude of mourning.

Matthew 5:5 *"Blessed are the meek, for they shall inherit the earth."*

The woman walked into my office in a terrible huff and stood in the doorway. "I want to talk to you!" she stated emphatically.

I tried to remain calm, but I could see the look on her face meant there would no doubt be trouble. "Sure, Melinda, come on in."

Melinda came in my office, making sure that she left the door open to my administrative assistant so everything could be heard.

"I don't like you. I know that you're aware of that. I don't like you," she stated.

"What's this about, Melinda?" I said as I felt the hair on the back of my neck begin to tingle.

"You think you're so smart. You think you're so great at this job. You're the best piano player ... you're the best vocalist ... you are so kind. Well, I don't buy into any of it! I didn't vote for you and I didn't want you here.

You're not real. You're just too kind! I don't believe you. I wanted you to know that!" she retorted and then stared at me with dark black eyes looking me over.

Let me retrace my steps so you can understand the situation I was in at the time of this episode. I had worked diligently to get a full-time position on staff at a neighboring church. When I say, diligently, I don't think that's a strong enough adjective. It was painstakingly long and tiresome as six months rolled by before the search committee, pastor, and elder board decided to offer me the position and have the church vote.

During these six months, I had shown up for meetings with every group in the church. I had led worship for them many times, been at staff meetings, prayer meetings, annual meetings, and felt "meeting-ed" out.

The pastor had called me in the early mornings and in the late evenings. I had met with several people for coffee to hear their problems and pray with them. I know what you're thinking ... but you didn't even have the job. I felt called to this church and called to these people. I loved them before I really even knew them, and I was following my father's advice when he told me, "Dress for the job, act like you have the job, and believe you will get the job."

It wasn't only that I wanted the position, but I had searched and searched for a fit, so I continued to use every ounce of self-control that I could muster up, and I remained calm and patient. I believed that God was in this with me.

Once the six months went by, the church had a vote. Because the former worship director was a part-time position, several of her friends wanted to prove their loyalty and put her into that role full time. Although she admittedly didn't want the job, they still wanted her. What did that do for me? It caused huge amounts of trouble.

The former director's friends began a diligent regime of calling all members and coercing them to vote "no" for me. I remember that one man had his friends call from their vacation in Florida, just so they could place their "no" vote.

I knew I was qualified for the job. I knew that I could make a difference in the position, but it didn't change the attitudes and human nature within the director's friends. Their attitude towards me was full of contempt, control, and callous.

The evening came for the big vote. Melinda was there in the front pew bellowing out all of the reasons that I was a poor candidate. No seminary degree (*for a worship director it's not really necessary*), I lived too far away (*12 miles*), I was too creative (*really?*), and wasn't I too busy with my three children? (*isn't everyone?*).

Can I tell you how I felt that night? Deep inside my heart and soul I wanted to stand on a chair and scream at the top of my lungs. I wanted to say, "Are you kidding me? You have had someone who can't play an instrument leading you for the past three years. You have bullied me, bullied your pastor, ignored your worship ministry, and lost attendees. Isn't it time to make a change?" But alas, I said nothing.

It was one of the hardest things I'd ever done. I listened to people critique me for what clothes I wore, what songs I chose, the color of my hair, the number of times I'd been there in the past six months ... or not been there, and on and on it went.

But deep inside of my being, I knew this was it, this was a make-me or break-me moment in time. I would need to take out a big God-size mirror and look at who I really was before God and these people. How would I act? How would I respond? What would it all mean if I could just remain calm, peace-filled, centered on God's will for my life, and have self-control?

My attitudes were everything that evening. It wasn't just important for the church to see who I was and could be, it wasn't just important for God to see me as I am, because He knew me inside and out, it was a test for my own self, a test that would allow me to see where I was on this journey and how mature I was. Was I Christ-like? Would I have self-control?

I was asked to step outside while the vote was made. My new friends voted and ran out into the hall to wait with me. Excitement and exhilaration flooded the hallway as they told me that they were so happy to have me for a new worship director.

The votes were counted and the majority were "no" votes. My heart sank and deep inside I was seething. All because a few people didn't want me, but wanted what they wanted, not what was good for their church, I was cast aside. Six months of meetings, prayer, preparation, and work were tossed out and I was devastated.

Again, it was a test for me. How would I respond? Tears began to well up in my eyes and I fought the urge to run from the room. I begged God for help. Not the kind of help you need when your sister is on the phone yelling at you because you forgot her birthday, but the kind of help you beg for when your world is crumbling.

I took a deep breath, stood up and looked around the room. I said nothing. I did nothing as though frozen in time. The pastor was angry with his face in his hands, the elders were whispering, and the mean people were joyously, but very quietly applauding the outcome. Yes, applauding. One friend began to sob in the back row.

Looking out at them, I said, "Thank you for this wonderful opportunity. God blessed me immensely as I enjoyed these past months working with you. I am confident that God will reveal to you the proper candidate and one that you are all in agreement with, and so I thank you and give you my warmest blessings." With that, I left the room.

The next day, the pastor and elders hired me as their interim for one year and I was hired with 100% vote. The mean people were fairly embarrassed and began attending another church after the first month that I served as interim worship director.

My point is that I could have chosen a sour attitude, a know-it-all attitude, or one that said, "Let me tell you what I think of all of you," but I reined it in and God blessed me for my efforts at being meek.

Back to that morning, I laid down everything I was working on and looked straight into Melinda's eyes. I said very gently with all the self control and meekness I could muster, "Melinda, I'm not sure what I've done here other than love you and support you, but somewhere in your life, someone like me must have hurt you really badly and for that I'm so very sorry. I am a real person with real feelings and I really do care about you."

Melinda burst into tears and spent the next hour talking about her horrific childhood. From that day forward, I had no more trouble with Melinda.

When Jesus is standing on the mountainside, delivering His beatitudes, He states, "Blessed (*happy or content*) are the meek, for they shall inherit the earth."

For years people have thought that being meek meant that you had to be wimpy. As a matter of fact, I believed they were one in the same. I thought meek meant quiet, giving in, and a big wimp.

On the contrary, meek means strength! If we look at the original form of the word *meek* in Greek, the word is *praus,* which has a deeper level of meaning. Webster's Dictionary states that the word *meek* means "*showing submissiveness and lack of initiative or will.*" But that's our English version of the word.

While observing this word *praus,* Help's Word-studies (© 1987, 2011 by Help's Ministries, Inc.) states, "*This difficult-to-translate root (pra-) means more than 'meek.' Biblical meekness is not weakness but rather refers to exercising God's strength under His control – i.e. demonstrating power without undue harshness.*"

Aristotle once said that *praus* is halfway between two extremes: on the one end there is someone who is too angry and on the other is someone who is not angry enough. *Praus* is directly in the middle, with a calm, patient, clear-minded, level-headed attitude. It's having an attitude that is gentle and submissive, but not a doormat.

Meek is also taken from the Hebrew root, *'ánaw,* which means *bending oneself down, humble, and gentle-like.*

Once again, Jesus is going against the ways of the world. He's not saying to lay down like a welcome mat and allow people to tread all over your spirit, but He's saying that *being meek* is a gentleness that has a strong inner self-control.

Why is this attitude essential in having a Christ-like persona?

 **Look Up: Numbers 12:3**

"*Moses was very meek, above all men on the face of the earth.*"

Sometimes being meek is just allowing someone else to be right.

Look Up: Matthew 11:29

"Take my yoke upon you and learn from me, for I am (meek) gentle and humble in heart, and you will find rest for your souls."

Sometimes being meek is just allowing someone else to be right. Maybe you're in a discussion and you have your opinion and your spouse has his. Maybe things aren't going so well. Your tendency will be to push until you get your way (*most of us are like this*). It's human nature. But observing Christ's attitude and being gentle and humble means that you will step aside and let your spouse "win" this time.

Look Up: Romans 12:16

"Do not set your mind on high things ... Do not be wise in your own opinion."

I remember meeting with my boss (*a pastor*) and talking with him about a very stubborn old man that continually told me that if I was smart, I'd do things his way. My boss looked at me, shook his head and said, "It's going to be a very long, hard walk, if you continue to stress every time someone in the congregation insists on their way. Pick and choose your battles when it's important and necessary, otherwise, use self control and be gentle with others." I used that as a mantra in my everyday world at church. It made all the difference in my attitude toward others.

Author of *The Practice of Godliness* (p. 181-182), Jerry Bridges states *"Both gentleness and meekness are born of power, not weakness. There is a pseudo-gentleness that is effeminate, and there is a pseudo-meekness that is cowardly. But a Christian is to be gentle and meek because those are Godlike virtues. We should never be afraid, therefore, that the gentleness of the Spirit means weakness of character. It takes strength, God's strength, to be truly gentle."*

In Galatians 5, we see what's known as the *Fruits of the Spirit* ... another set of "attitudes" for us to grasp, embrace and live by. You will notice that the same spirit of meekness, or gentleness and self-control is listed as an attribute.

 **Look Up: Galatians 5:22-23, 25**

"But the fruit of the Spirit is love, joy, peace, patience, kindness, goodness, faithfulness, gentleness and self-control ... Since we live by the Spirit, let us keep in step with the Spirit."

Being meek is an attitude of response. How do you treat others and how do you respond to them when you're in a tough situation? Human nature will tell you to snap back, to criticize, or even to defend yourself. Jesus shows us over and over in scripture that He remains in self-control and gentle in spirit.

 **Look Up: Psalm 25:9**

"The meek will he guide in judgment: and the meek will he teach his way."

Working on this attitude will be a daily adventure! Warren Wiersbe says, "Meekness is power under control." Here are some steps to help you be power-filled and grasp self-control.

 **STEP ONE: *Be. patient* with those around you**

Ephesians 4:2, "Be completely humble and gentle; be patient, bearing with one another in love."

Colossians 3:12, "Therefore, as God's chosen people, holy and dearly loved, clothe yourselves with compassion, kindness, humility, gentleness and patience."

Colossians 3:8, "But now you must rid yourselves of all such things as these: anger, rage, malice, slander, and filthy language from your lips."

STEP TWO: ***Be. tolerant*** **of others' opinions by listening and caring about what they think**

Philippians 2:3, "Do nothing out of selfish ambition or vain conceit, but in humility consider others better than yourselves."

James 3:17, "But the wisdom that comes from heaven is first of all pure; then peace-loving, considerate, submissive, full of mercy and good fruit, impartial and sincere."

Romans 12:10, "Be devoted to one another in brotherly love."

STEP THREE: ***Be. forgiving*** **when others hurt you and remain gentle in spirit**

Matthew 6:12, "Forgive us our debts as we forgive our debtors."

Romans 12: 17, "Do not repay anyone evil for evil."

Colossians 3:13, "Bear with each other and forgive whatever grievances you may have against one another. Forgive as the Lord forgave you."

STEP FOUR: *Be. calm* when others come against you in an attack mode

Romans 12:14, "Bless those who persecute you; bless and do not curse."

Romans 12:18, "If it is possible, as far as it depends on you, live at peace with everyone."

II Timothy 2:24, "And the Lord's servant must not quarrel; instead, he must be kind to everyone, able to teach, not resentful."

Blessed are the gentle. Blessed are the meek. Blessed are we when we give a huge dose of patience to someone who bugs us. Blessed are we when we can apply Godly attitudes to our everyday circumstances. Blessed are we when people think we're just too nice.

Questions:

1. Share a situation where you were able to display self-control.

2. Do you believe it's feasible to be gentle and not be pushed around? Explain your view.

3. How do you balance your anger and irritability with patience and being meek to others?

4. Share a time you prayed for someone who hurt you or created trouble for you.

Look Up:

1. **Proverbs 16.18-19**
2. **I Peter 3:4**
3. **James 1:21-25**
4. **James 4:6-10**

Songs:

Hymn- *"I Stand Amazed"*

Contemporary - *"I Could Sing of Your Love Forever" (Martin Smith)*

Closing Prayer:

Dear Jesus, sometimes it's difficult
to be gentle to others
who may be unkind or pushing me
and making me feel threatened or hurt.
Please help me to be loving
and kind today.

Help me to learn to balance being
in control of my emotions
and being Christ-like
in my attitudes towards others.
I cannot do this without Your Spirit
and His help.

In Jesus' Name, *Amen.*

CHAPTER 4

Those Who Hunger & Thirst After Righteousness 

"God's plan is for you to become the best version of you, but right now there are two versions of you. There is the you God made you to be and the you that currently exists. What do you do with the gap?"

John Ortberg

Be. God-Seeking Be. Encouraged Be. Blessed

The Buzz: Last week we learned that "those who are meek" means we are to have an attitude of self-control.

Matthew 5:6 *"Blessed are those who hunger and thirst after righteousness for they will be filled."*

When I was a little girl, we lived in southwest Iowa. My mother was a stay-at-home mom until I was in junior high, and my father worked as a college professor. Every evening, my mother served a delicious meal, usually leaving leftovers for our homemade lunches for school. She never sent us out the door without a fabulous big breakfast.

As a child, I did a lot of grumbling. My mother was way ahead of her time, and the Food Network would have been very proud of her. My mother would spend her days baking beautiful brown loaves of rye bread, white parker house rolls, dilly bread with fresh dill from the garden, and homemade sunflower seed cookies.

Morning after morning, we awoke to buckwheat pancakes, cornmeal mush, or long cooking oatmeal with honey from the neighbors beehive. Night after night, we would sit down to fresh vegetables from the garden (*or her canned goods in the winter months*), delicate slices of roast beef, and scalloped potatoes with rosemary. Everything on the table was wonderfully delicious to the palette.

My father was adamant about our family's time together, and our family meals were mandatory. We were never allowed to leave the table until everyone was finished and we had asked to be dismissed.

Once I reached junior high, I would hide in the corner when it came time for school lunch. Because my mother packed our lunches, I brought homemade whole wheat bread slathered with REAL peanut butter, wrapped in wax paper, along with some fresh fruit, and usually a date nut cookie or some other homemade kind of dessert.

The other children would snicker as they would happily lay out their Wonder bread with Jiffy peanut butter, Lays potato chips, and Hostess Twinkies. I would moan and groan as I would open up my thermos to homemade grape juice or milk (*at least I felt like I fit in with my Peanuts lunchbox!*).

I would say over and over that I would give anything for a piece of that plastic texture cheese or some Oscar Mayer bologna. Instead, it was some pepper jack cheese or homemade sausage on my sandwich.

As time went by, I realized that as we sat at our dinner table, my family and I were having lively conversations about life, politics, the Bible, and how to live a healthy life. The old green table that pulled out as far and long as any table I'd ever seen became a comfort to me. There, we met each other and there, we met with God.

Daddy would come home from the college and ask my sister and me to help grade papers. We'd spread things out on that old green table. Mom would bring in some homemade pizza and sometimes we'd even invite neighborhood kids over to share our suppers.

As kids experienced my mother's food, they'd begin to ask me at lunchtime if they could trade their Twinkie for Mom's cookies, or their Wonder bread for my mom's homemade dilly bread. I began to accept, long for, and feel appreciative of the healthy food my mother served. Previously, I had rejected the healthy food but now I loved it.

The years passed by, and my mother, now eighty-two, no longer cooks her extravagant and time-consuming homemade foods. I long for that good, wholesome way of eating, just as I longed for the old green table. Much to my surprise, the last time I visited Mom, she took my hand and led me downstairs to the corner and said, "Would you and Dean like the old green table?"

"Would I?" I smiled and responded, "Of course!"

The table was a turning point in my life, because when my father passed away a few years ago, I couldn't quite fill the void of missing him, but that old green table brought me comfort, that table where I learned to yearn for God's Word and good food. And then, it dawned on me; why not continue to use this table as it was always used? Why not continue its heritage? I began to get up every morning and seek God's Word, just as my folks did, right there at that old green farm table.

I created a new daily habit. Every morning I awake, grab my cup of coffee, my study Bible and devotional, and sit in the big captain's chair on the end of that wonderful old green table. I would face the other captain's chair far at the other end, and prepare myself for a breakfast with God. I would fill up on good earthly food, and good spiritual food from God's Word.

With my running list of prayer requests in front of me and my English muffin topped with melted butter, I would release my thoughts, emotions, and needs before a Mighty God. I'd eat, read, worship, and then look down at the end of the table and say to God, "Now it's your turn. You tell me what you want me to know. You teach me what I need to learn for today. You order my steps, dear Father." As I read the words that were in my Bible, I'd soak them into the depths of my soul, the crevices of the closets of my mind, and wait on Him. I thought about the world around me. I thought about how every morning we are thrust onto the pathway of our lives. We juggle the jobs, the children, the church, and our faith. What will drop today? What will fall to the ground as we cannot carry it all? What is it that is keeping all of us so busy that we don't have time for God? He tells us in Proverbs "listen well to My words because those people who listen live ... *really live*."

Don't we really want to live? We don't want to walk through this life being too busy to enjoy each day. I certainly don't want to be too busy for the God who loves me and sent His Son for me.

We don't need hours upon hours; we just need some designated time to realize that hungering for God means filling up on life. It's His nourishment for us. Breakfast on the go ... Breakfast of Champions ... Breakfast at Tiffany's ...who cares ...we can make it *Breakfast with God.*

> When we look at the attitude of the heart that says we are to hunger and thirst after righteousness, we realize that Jesus is emphasizing a relentless pursuit of a need for more of God.

When we look at the attitude of the heart that says we are to hunger and thirst after righteousness, we realize that Jesus is emphasizing a relentless pursuit of a need for more of God. But it isn't enough to seek God by just being hungry and thirsty for Him. We must be hungering and thirsting after righteousness. That's seeking God to live a Godly life, a life filled with days that bring honor and glory to God, not sin and strife.

Are you committed to being hungry and thirsty for more of God? Chuck Swindoll says, "*Make a plan now to keep a daily appointment with God. The enemy is going to tell you to set it aside, but you must carve out the time. If you're too busy to meet with the Lord, friend, then you are simply too busy.*"

Look Up: Proverbs 4:20-23

"Dear friend, listen well to my words; tune your ears to My voice. Keep My message in plain view at all times. Concentrate! Learn it by heart! Those who discover these words, live, really live, body and soul, they're bursting with health. Keep vigilant watch over your heart: that's where life starts" (MSG).

Jesus is looking for a heart attitude that says, "I need You. I don't have it all, and actually, I don't have anything, so I'm seeking You for my very breath and existence." The blessing isn't for those who have arrived, but for those who are continually seeking (*hungering and thirsting*) after God. They are continually moving forward, bettering themselves by filling up on God.

Look Up: Isaiah 58:10

"I will always show you where to go; I'll give you a full life in the emptiest of places" (MSG).

If we are to remain Christ-like, we need to be filling up daily on God, on talking with Him, meeting with Him, reading His Word, listening to His voice through His Word, Godly music, Godly books, and Christian friends and family. How can we become like Him if we know nothing about Him? It is an ongoing relationship.

Charles Spurgeon states, "*To hunger after righteousness is a sign of spiritual life. Nobody who was spiritually dead ever did this ... If you hunger and thirst after righteousness, you are spiritually alive ... When the Spirit of God has changed our nature, that new nature hungers and thirsts after righteousness. The old nature never did, never could, and never would do so.*"

Our flesh will never want to do the right thing, seek God diligently, or seek after righteousness. Webster's dictionary says that *righteousness* means "*always behaving according to a religious or moral code.*" *Always* means "*throughout all past time or all future time, or for as long as anyone can remember.*" Righteousness isn't something we're going to be able to seek on our own. We need a big dose of God's help!

Look Up: Psalm 63:1

"*God-You're my God! I can't get enough of You! I've worked up such hunger and thirst for God, traveling across dry and weary deserts*" *(MSG).*

If we align our thoughts, our actions, and our will with God's Word and His desires for us to live a better life, then we will fall in line with hungering and thirsting after righteousness.

I think back on the days of childhood where my own taste would have preferred those things that were not healthy for me. After all, they looked good and tasted good, but they never really satisfied me. Have one Twinkie, want fourteen more! Gobble down a sunflower seed cookie, and the rich sweetness of the honey and meaty satisfaction of the nuts would do the trick of satisfying after one cookie alone!

Just as when we eat unhealthy snacks, when we seek the world, we are left discontent. Alternately, the Word of God is like the cookie bursting with health. When we seek God and His Word and ways, we are filled to the brim, left feeling satisfied.

 **Look Up: Isaiah 58:11**

"The Lord will guide you always; He will satisfy your needs in a sun-scorched land and will strengthen your frame. You will be like a well-watered garden, like a spring whose waters never fail."

If we got up in the morning and decided that once and for all we would drink a big glass of water, eat some bacon, eggs and toast, and be satisfied and full for the rest of our lives, that would be an absurd way of thinking. As humans, we must continually eat to have strength to be alive and survive. Why should we think that we could meet with God, seek Him only once and a while, and be satisfied?

Mother Teresa once said, *"The poverty in the West is a different kind of poverty, it is not only a poverty of loneliness but also of spirituality. There's a hunger for love, as there is a hunger for God."*

Our hunger and our passions are revealed as what is most important to us. Perhaps it's our children, or our job, or even our houses or possessions. But whatever you deem the most valuable in your life, will be where your passion lies. If your passion becomes God, you will do whatever it takes to desire Him, to seek Him, to meet with Him, and to learn more about Him and how to be like Him.

 **Look Up: II Chronicles 15:2**

"The Lord is with you when you are with Him. If you seek Him, He will be found by you."

Seeking after righteousness is an attitude of action. Will we make time for God, who is the author of our lives? Human nature tells us that our time should be spent on our actions. Why would we want to seek God and righteousness? To be more like Him of course!

Developing this attitude will be a daily necessity in your life. Stephen Covey, the author of *The Seven Habits of Highly Effective People* says, *"The essence of effective time and life management is to organize and execute around priorities."* Remember that whatever we value most in life becomes our priority.

Here are some steps that will help you to develop a daily routine with God.

STEP ONE: *Be. God seeking* and submit everything to Him, including your time

Psalm 63:1, "God-You're my God! I can't get enough of You! I've worked up such hunger thirst for God, traveling across dry and weary deserts" *(MSG).*

Psalm 42:1-2, "As a deer pants for flowing streams, so pants my soul for you, O God. My soul thirsts for God, for the living God."

Psalm 63:1, "O God, you are my God; earnestly I seek you; my soul thirsts for you; my flesh faints for you, as in a dry and weary land where there is no water."

 **STEP TWO:** ***Make a list*** **of priorities and passions**

Ephesians 5:15-16, "Be very careful, then, how you live - not as unwise but as wise, making the most of every opportunity, because the days are evil."

Proverbs 16:3, "Put God in charge of your work. Then what you have planned will take place" *(MSG).*

Psalm 39:4-5, "Show me, O Lord, my life's end and the number of my days; let me know how fleeting is my life. You have made my days a mere handbreadth; the span of my years is as nothing before you. Each man's life is but a breath."

STEP THREE: ***Meet with God*** **regularly and review your progress**

Psalm 119:105, "Thy Word is a lamp unto my feet and a light onto my path."

John 4:14, "... but whoever drinks the water I give them will never thirst. Indeed, the water I give them will become in them a spring of water welling up to eternal life."

Matthew 6:33, "But seek first his kingdom and his righteousness, and all these things will be given to you as well."

STEP FOUR: ***Be. encouraged*** **and remain consistent**

Proverbs 16:3, "Commit to the Lord whatever you do, and your plans will succeed."

Psalm 33:11, “But the plans of the Lord stand firm forever, the purposes of his heart through all generations.”

Psalm 107:9,“ ... for He satisfies the thirsty and fills the hungry with good things.”

Blessed are the ones who seek God and meet with Him regularly. Blessed are those who are hungry for more of God, who are thirsting for righteousness and doing things God’s way. Blessed are we when we’re sitting at our big green tables, soaking up the Word of God and His goodness. When we take time to read God’s Word, we know more about God, and subsequently we know more about how much we need Him.

“Blessed the man, blessed the woman, who listens to Me, awake and ready for Me each morning, alert and responsive as I start my day’s work. When you find Me, you find life, real life” Proverbs 8:34-35 *(MSG)*.

Questions:

1. Do you have a regular set time to meet with God, pray, and read your Bible? Are you consistent with this?

2. Do you find that it’s difficult to make time for studying God’s Word or even attend church?

3. How can you make God more of a priority in your life?

4. What are some ways that you can encourage your family and friends to make time for God?

 **Look Up:**

1. **Psalm 107:9**
2. **Isaiah 49:10**
3. **I Peter 2:24**
4. **II Corinthians 5:21**

 **Songs:**

Hymn - "*Come Thou Fount*"

Contemporary - "*Breathe*" *(Marie Barnett)*

Closing Prayer:

Dear Jesus, help me
to have the desire
to seek you diligently,
with every fiber of my being,
on a daily basis.

I pray that You will give me
the wisdom and knowledge
to know how to study Your Word
and absorb its truths.

Allow me to learn
and grow in Your Word
and Your ways.
In Jesus' Name, *Amen.*

CHAPTER 5

Merciful

"Grace answers to the undeserving;
mercy answers to the miserable!"

D.A. Carson

Be. Compassionate   Be. Sympathetic   Be. Blessed

The Buzz: Last week we learned that "those who hunger and thirst after righteousness" means that we are to have an attitude that seeks God and hungers after Him and Godly things.

Matthew 5:7 *"Blessed are the merciful, for they shall be shown mercy."*

The young man sat next to his wife and looked across the table at me. Leo was quiet and downcast as he sipped steaming hot coffee from an old white cup and saucer. I looked around the room while I waited for him to respond. It had been almost three days since I had arrived in Poland on a mission trip, and I was staying with Leo and his wife of two years.

The couple was in their early twenties and I was old enough to be their mother. Fortunately, the church had partnered me together with this young couple, and although many of my fellow team members were scattered hither and yonder staying with others who were not as polished in the English language, I would smile as this young couple would carefully formulate their words when answering my questions.

Leo and his wife went to the church where we were helping, and also served at the children's camp, but I noticed a deep, dark sadness that permeated Leo's heart day after day. I finally broke that darkness by asking him, "Leo, I sense that there is something troubling you. Could I pray with you?"

In broken English Leo finally answered, "Yes, please pray."

The first few days had zipped by as we served together at the church. A feeling of comfort began to settle in around the team and around Leo, his wife, and me, as we fixed the church in the day, and led worship services at night. But I could sense something stirring in the soul of my new friend, and I felt a sense of urgency to help him.

Another day passed by and that evening the three of us settled into the tiny little apartment where the couple lived. While I was getting my music prepared for the next day, they asked if they could chat with me. Each night they had come into my room and sat at the end of my bed like they were little children. I'd talk with them about their day and we'd talk about the United States, what it was like to live in Poland, and then I'd pray for them. This night was different. I could feel it.

Leo began by saying that he trusted no one but his wife and his pastor. With teary eyes and a choked voice, he said to me, "Now I trust you." I thanked him and listened. I knew exactly what it was like to trust no one. I trusted God and my parents. That was it.

Leo began his story and, every so often, his wife would pat his hand so he could gather courage and continue. Leo told me that when he was a small boy his father died. A couple of years later, his mother remarried a man who was very violent and angry. Whenever Leo would do a simple thing that would be wrong, he was beaten.

After he reached the age of twelve, he started heading out to the streets after school, so that he could avoid the risk of another beating. The street kids were wild and tough and started offering him drugs and alcohol. He felt like it took away the sting of the loss he felt and the pain of the beatings he would receive.

A couple of years went by and the step-father began to abuse Leo's little brother as well. Leo never went into detail, but I could sense it wasn't just mental and physical abuse. Leo packed a few clothes in a backpack and headed out to live on the streets. At age fourteen, he wasn't ready for what he would find.

To stay alive, Leo told me that he had to engage in a lifestyle filled with prostitution and drug errands. The story stopped as Leo began to sob. I got up and moved to the edge of the bed near him and his wife. I wrapped my arms around him, hugged and comforted him until he could continue.

Leo went on to tell me that one bright sunny autumn day, a young schoolmate from his old neighborhood found him on the street and said, "Your grandmother sent me. Your mom is dying of cancer. She wants you with her. She is at the hospital."

Leo replied, "I cannot see her, I cannot go to her. I am too ashamed. Leave me alone!"

Two days later, the young man came back and found him. He said, "Leo, your grandmother sent me back. She said that it doesn't matter what you've done. Come home."

Leo told me about his shame and his fears. He could not see his mother or his grandmother, who were both Godly upright women, after the lifestyle he'd lived over that past year. He looked at me and said, "I trusted no one. Everyone was out for themselves. Food was hard to come by, and my sin was great to be able to get my food. I could not go back. I was like a leper."

But something changed inside of Leo and he felt called to his mother's side. He did not know that his mom and grandmother had the entire church praying for him. He walked into his mother's hospital room and saw her shriveled up under the hospital covers. Her eyes lit up as she held out a frail little hand. "My baby!" she said. "Come here."

As Leo moved across the room and hugged his mother, they both cried. He said, "I have no life, Mama, I have no life."

His mother told him that day that he needed to come home. The step-father had left them, the grandmother had moved in, and the church was helping them. It was safe now to come home. She understood how he felt because when he left, the step-dad had turned the abuse towards her and the little brother. She had kicked him out. She knew what it was like to be hungry, to be cold, and to be worried about what was happening next.

Leo told me he would never forget what his mother did next. She said, "I have something for you." She reached around the back of her neck and unclasped her necklace. It was a small cross made of amber, which is prevalent in his country. Leo explained to me that amber is a light golden-reddish color gemstone formed by the fossilization of tree sap around pieces of leaves, twigs, and insects (*including bees*!). She handed the cross to him.

"I cannot take your cross, Mama." Leo said. His mother insisted that he take it from her.

"All is forgiven, Leo. See this cross? Look at the little bug inside of it, and yet the beauty of the stone encompasses the bug. That is God's love, forgiveness, and mercy for you and me. It is all-encompassing. The bug has become beautiful now, because of the cross."

Leo stopped his story and looked up at me. "I lived a life of shame until then. I moved back home and my mama died. I changed my life. Still, I trust no one, but you are like my mama. You are kind, you are gentle, and you are full of mercy."

He reached into his pocket and pulled out the chain with the cross. He said to me, "Here, you have it. You be reminded of me and my story and how God used you to help me trust another person. Maybe this will help me continue to trust again."

I have that cross in my jewelry box at home. I carry it with me when I talk to all age groups, from young kids to old grandparents. That story, that cross, never cease to speak the truth to me and to those who hear about mercy and grace. Grace is a loving response when that love is undeserved. But mercy, well, mercy is a loving response prompted by someone else's misery and helplessness.

The attitude that Christ is teaching about in Matthew 5:7 is simply this: someone who is merciful will be someone who has a heart attitude of mercy. A mercy-filled individual will be focused on those around him/her, not oneself. To be merciful implies a focus on what's happening around us, and what's happening to others physically, emotionally and spiritually. When we are merciful, we become aware of the suffering and the needs of those who are in our personal "world" of neighborhoods, workplaces, families, and friends, and we help to meet the needs of those individuals.

Of course we can always show mercy to the world at large, but it must start in the small scope of our everyday lives.

Look Up: John 15:12

"This is my commandment, that you love one another as I have loved you."

The Greek word *eleemon* means the same thing as the English word *merciful* used in Matthew 5:7, which essentially mean the same thing, *showing compassion to somebody.* However, many theologians believe that Jesus spoke in Aramaic so the word He would have used is the Hebrew and Aramaic *chesed.*

William Barclay's *Daily Study Bible* commentary on Matthew regarding the word, *mercy*, states: *"It does not mean only to sympathize with a person in the popular sense of the term; it does not mean simply to feel sorry for some in trouble.* Chesedh [sic], mercy, *means the ability to get right inside the other person's skin ... this is much more than an emotional wave of pity; clearly this demands a quite deliberate effort of the mind and of the will. It denotes a sympathy which is not given, as it were, from outside, but which comes from a deliberate identification with the other person, until we see things as he sees them, and feel things as he feels them. This is* sympathy *in the literal sense of the word.* Sympathy *is derived from two Greek words,* syn *which means* 'together with', *and* paschein *which means* 'to experience or to suffer.' Sympathy *means* 'experiencing things together with the other person,' *literally going through what he is going through."*

This is mercy. This is the kind of mercy that Jesus is referring to ... the kind of mercy that crawls inside the skin of another and experiences his feelings, his hurt and pain, and sees from that hurting person's perspective. It is an attitude that puts on a deep sense of compassion for those around us.

Jesus gives us a great example of what mercy looks like in the story of the Good Samaritan. In this story, Jesus gives three examples of people who were very much aware of the condition of a beaten man, lying on the side of the road. Two pass by him, and one stops to show mercy.

Look Up: Luke 10:30-37

" In reply Jesus said: 'A man was going down from Jerusalem to Jericho, when he was attacked by robbers. They stripped him of his clothes, beat him and went away, leaving him half dead. A priest happened to be going down the same road, and when he saw the man, he passed by on the other side. So too, a Levite, when he came to the place and saw him, passed by on the other side. But a Samaritan, as he traveled, came where the man was; and when he saw him, he took pity on him. He went to him and bandaged his wounds, pouring on oil and wine. Then he put the man on his own donkey, brought him to an inn and took care of him. The next day he took out two denarii and gave them to the innkeeper. 'Look after him,' he said, 'and when I return, I will reimburse you for any extra expense you may have.'
"'Which of these three do you think was a neighbor to the man who fell into the hands of robbers?'
"The expert in the law replied, 'The one who had mercy on him.'
"Jesus told him, 'Go and do likewise.'"

The road from Jerusalem to Jericho was a very dangerous road to travel. The winding and meandering road made it easy for robbers to hide and prepare an attack.

Martin Luther King, Jr. said this about the road, *"In the days of Jesus it came to be known as the 'Bloody Pass.' And you know, it's possible that the priest and the Levite looked over that man on the ground and wondered if the robbers were still around. Or it's possible that they felt that the man on the ground was merely faking, and he was acting like he had been robbed and hurt in order to seize them over there, lure them there for quick and easy seizure. And so the first question that the priest asked, the first question that the Levite asked was, 'If I stop to help this man, what will happen to me?' But then the Good Samaritan came by, and he reversed the question: 'If I do not stop to help this man, what will happen to him?'"*

Samaritans were hated by Jesus' audience. Can you imagine the response that day as Luke describes it in chapter 10 and as Jesus used this example? A priest, a Levite, and a Samaritan are all given the same opportunity to show mercy. The Samaritan puts himself in the place of the beaten man on the side of the road. He not only stops to help, but he "takes pity on him." He shows mercy. The Samaritan bandages up the man's wounds, puts him on his own donkey and carries him to the inn. He pays for the overnight stay and says anything else he needs, just put it on my bill. What does Jesus say? "Go and do likewise." Just do it. Have mercy. Be compassionate. Show that you care.

Look Up: Colossians 3:12-14

"Therefore, as the elect of God, holy and beloved, put on tender mercies, kindness, humbleness of mind, meekness, longsuffering; bearing with one another, and forgiving one another, if anyone has a complaint against another; even as Christ forgave you, so you also must do. But above all these things put on love, which is the bond of perfection."

If we want to show others mercy, we must experience need, hurt, and brokenness. I can't begin to tell you how many times I wish that I could avoid pain and sorrow. But what I've learned in my lifetime is that pain and sorrow bring us to a much deeper level of compassion for others.

When we've experienced something, we can understand how that other person feels, who is now going through it. We can reach out and empathize, sympathize, and we have wisdom about what will or will not bring comfort.

 **Look Up: II Corinthians 1:3-5**

"Praise be to the God and Father of our Lord Jesus Christ, who comforts us in all our troubles, so that we can comfort those in any trouble with the comfort we ourselves have received from God. For just as the sufferings of Christ flow over into our lives, so also through Christ our comfort overflows."

Mercy doesn't just show up when someone is in need of physical or emotional help, but mercy also needs to arise out of our souls when we feel someone doesn't deserve our mercy. Mercy isn't a choice, it's a heart attitude. We can be merciful, even when we don't feel like it or want to give mercy.

Let's face it; there are people in our lives who have been hurtful. I know that. You know that. And then it happens ... God allows that hurtful person to be in a place of vulnerability where you must decide how you will respond. I call it "the switch." God uses whatever circumstances that works in their lives to allow them to see what they've done to you, or to others. The next thing you know, they are in need of comfort, mercy, or help. What happens then? How do you respond?

My favorite example of this kind of mercy comes from a story that Corrie Ten Boom, a prisoner of war during World War II, tells. Here is an excerpt:

"... that's when I saw him, working his way forward against the others. One moment I saw the overcoat and the brown hat; the next, a blue uniform and a visored cap with its skull and crossbones. It came back

with a rush: the huge room with its harsh overhead lights, the pathetic pile of dresses and shoes in the center of the floor, the shame of walking naked past this man.

"Betsie and I had been arrested for concealing Jews in our home during the Nazi occupation of Holland; this man had been a guard at Ravensbruck concentration camp where we were sent ...

"'You mentioned Ravensbruck in your talk' he was saying. 'I was a guard in there.' No, he did not remember me. 'But since that time,' he went on, 'I have become a Christian. I know that God has forgiven me for the cruel things I did there, but I would like to hear it from your lips as well. Fraulein,' his hand came out, ... 'will you forgive me?'

"And I stood there — I whose sins had every day to be forgiven — and could not. Betsie had died in that place — could he erase her slow terrible death simply for the asking?

"It could not have been many seconds that he stood there, hand held out, but to me it seemed hours as I wrestled with the most difficult thing I had ever had to do.

"For I had to do it — I knew that. The message that God forgives has a prior condition: that we forgive those who have injured us. 'If you do not forgive men their trespasses,' Jesus says, 'neither will your Father in heaven forgive your trespasses' ...

"And still I stood there with the coldness clutching my heart. But forgiveness is not an emotion — I knew that too. Forgiveness is an act of the will, and the will can function regardless of the temperature of the heart. 'Jesus, help me!' I prayed silently. 'I can lift my hand, I can do that much. You supply the feeling.'

" 'I forgive you, brother!' I cried. 'With all my heart!'

Mercy consists of responding to the needs of others and doing it with an attitude that says, "How can I help?"

"For a long moment we grasped each other's hands, the former guard and the former prisoner. I had never known God's love so intensely as I did then."

Mercy consists of responding to the needs of others and doing it with an attitude that says, "How can I help?" It's compassion and caring. It's sympathy and providing relief. In this passage, *mercy* is a verb ... it's an *action*. It needs to be the attitude that follows the other *be.attitudes* and we must respond to the changes that are taking place in our hearts when we commit to God that we want His attitudes to reside in our hearts, souls, and minds.

Once we have emptied ourselves of pride and embraced humility (*Matthew 5:3*), we take on an attitude of mourning for our sins and being honest before God (*Matthew 5:4*). After we have understood being meek, and having the attitude of self control (*Matthew 5:5)* we begin to see that we are emptied of ourselves and our human attitudes. Now, we're taking on Christ's attitudes. Emptiness creates a void where God can fill us up and we move on to hungering and thirsting after righteousness (*Matthew 5:6*).

The next three attitudes will be the ones that fill the empty soul with God-attitudes. This verse is mercy *(Matthew 5:7)* and in the next verses *(Matthew 5:8)* we will learn about purity (*Matthew 5:8*) and peacemaking (*Matthew 5:9*). Mercy is the first thing we will fill up on and we learn it from our best example ... *Jesus.*

*" ... Mercy is our only hope from God, and our neighbors' only hope from us as well" (*Peter Kreeft, *Back to Virtue).*

Look Up: Ephesians 1:7

"He is so rich in kindness and grace that he purchased our freedom with the blood of his Son and forgave our sins."

Here are some steps that will help you to focus on those around you who are desperately in need of mercy.

STEP ONE: *Be. aware* of those around you

Romans 12:9-10, "Love must be sincere. Hate what is evil; cling to what is good. Be devoted to one another in brotherly love. Honor one another above yourselves."

Philippians 2:3-4, "Do nothing from selfish, empty conceit, but with humility of mind regard one another as more important than yourself; do not merely look out for your own personal interests, but also for the interest of others."

John 13:34-35, "A new commandment I give to you, that you love one another: just as I have loved you, you also are to love one another. By this all people will know that you are my disciples, if you have love for one another."

STEP TWO: *Be. compassionate*

Psalm 147:3, "He heals the brokenhearted, and binds up their wounds."

Ephesians 4:2, "Be completely humble and gentle; be patient, bearing with one another in love."

I John 3:18, "Little children, let us not love with word or with tongue, but in deed and truth."

STEP THREE: *Be. forgiving*

Colossians 3:13, "Make allowance for each other's faults, and forgive anyone who offends you. Remember, the Lord forgave you, so you must forgive others."

James 5:16, "Confess your faults one to another, and pray one for another, that ye may be healed."

Mark 11:25, "And when ye stand praying, forgive, if ye have ought against any: that your Father also which is in heaven may forgive you your trespasses."

STEP FOUR: *Be. a blessing* to others

Ephesians 4:32, "Instead, be kind to each other, tenderhearted, forgiving one another, just as God through Christ has forgiven you."

James 2:13, "For judgment will be merciless to one who has shown no mercy; mercy triumphs over judgment."

II Samuel 22:26, "With the merciful You will show Yourself merciful" *(ESV).*

Blessed are the ones who show mercy, kindness, and love to those around them. Blessed are those who know they are the little bug inside the beautiful amber cross, and rejoice in the forgiveness of the Savior. Blessed are those who were once lost and are now found because of

God's grace. Blessed are we when we cannot muster up the courage to be mercy-filled, but we rely on God's power and strength to help us. Blessed are we when we remember: To embrace the attitude of mercy is to embrace the whole premise of the cross.

Questions:

1. Would you consider yourself someone who is full of mercy?

2. Give examples of how you reach out to those around you and bring encouragement, comfort, hope and relief?

3. When was the last time someone showed you mercy? Have you ever struggled with showing someone mercy because they have hurt you?

4. What is the difference between grace and mercy?

Look Up:

1. **Psalm 86:5-7**

2. **Psalm 103:6-13**

3. **Psalm 136:1**

4. **Luke 6:37-38**

Songs:

Hymn - "*What a Friend We Have In Jesus*"

Contemporary - "*Sing of Our God*" *(Jamgochian)*

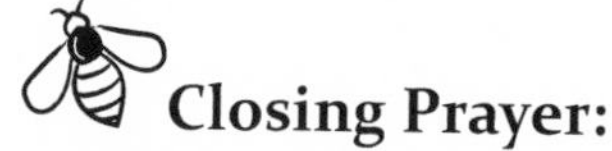

Closing Prayer:

Dear Jesus, help me to look outside of myself
at those around me.
Help me to see their needs
and listen for their sufferings.
Allow me to be the hands and feet of Christ,
by doling out large doses of mercy.

Give me strength to show compassion
and wisdom to know what to say and what to do.
For the times when I am challenged
to provide a grace-filled, merciful attitude,
fill me with your love
and pour me out like a vase full of God-water.

Help me to be a blessing to others.
In Jesus' Name, *Amen.*

CHAPTER 6

Pure In Heart

"Like a spring of pure water, God's peace in our hearts brings cleansing and refreshment to our minds and bodies."

Billy Graham

Be. Repentant   Be. Selfless   Be. Blessed

The Buzz: Last week we learned that God's desire for us is that we would have an attitude of compassion and mercy for those around us.

Matthew 5:8 *"Blessed are the pure in heart, for they will see God."*

I got up from my chair feeling a bit wobbly, as the realization of what just happened washed over me like a bucket of cold water.

Newly hired to my position as worship director at the church, the pastor had cheerfully called me in to announce that we were headed across the world on a mission trip. He would need me to lead worship in a foreign country. He asked me three things: 1) to find a team of five musicians 2) to raise funds 3) to be ready to go in sixteen days.

It wasn't the list of things to do that got me upset, it was my fear of flying. I bravely nodded my head and walked out the door, trying to make it to my office before I began to engage in a frenzied fit of panic.

Somehow I told myself everything would be okay because no one would want to go. Four days later, five people from my team had come into my office to announce they could hardly wait to get on the plane and head across the world with me. Who were these people (*so much for relying on the team's rejection to help me out*)? I checked that excuse off of my list and waited to see what would happen next. I still had the excuse that I couldn't raise that kind of money in a short time frame.

The very next day, my assistant brought in the mail, only to reveal that an old junior high friend had mailed a check for the full amount so that I could go on the trip. Ugh! I'd have to go. I began my preparation for this trip. I packed several bottles of Tylenol (*for headaches from worry*), several boxes of Pepto-Bismol (*for all of the sickness I'd experience on the so-said-plane*), music with a CD player (*to keep my mind busy),* and several crosses (*to wear around my neck to remember Christ's sacrifice for me).*

The dreaded day arrived and my team drove to the airport, boarded the plane, and I saw *him*. There he was, standing proudly at the top of the stairs, sporting a neat pressed, white uniform and white shoes. His smile was as white as his shoes, and as the *Captain* of the plane, he was welcoming people aboard.

I quickly faced him, said good morning and asked him, "How are you feeling today? Did you sleep well last night?"

My girlfriends shoved me down the aisle and quickly said to me, "You can't ask him that!" There were thirteen of us in our church group, and I felt that I would be okay, knowing that we were sitting in the front of the plane. Oh, wait! It was the middle. No, now we were moving all the way to the back row. My pastor continued to smile at me. I tried to look the other way for fear he'd figure out I was terrified.

I sat down with a girlfriend on each side of me, my ice tea in tow (*back then they let you bring on your own microwave if you wanted),* a few dozen snacks (*alright it was a box of Cheezits*) and my CD player. Armed with many books and magazines, I told myself I could do it ... just thirteen more hours. Well, once the plane took off it would be thirteen more hours.

The plane pulled out and I began to moan and groan. Until my friends told me we were still on the ground. Because it was mid-November, the weather was very cold, chilly, and ... *winter*. Not the best time to be traveling across the world.

About two hours into our journey it began, something known as *turbulence*. I'm scared. By now, my friends are scared. I tell everyone I will not become terrified until I see the flight attendant becoming nervous. Just at that moment, she sat down across from us, put on her seatbelt and crossed herself. Now I'm worried.

The plane began to flail back and forth, and I did the only thing that a nervous, scared, *sure-that-we-are-going-to-die-any-minute* worship director knows how to do. I unfastened my seatbelt, stood and said, "Since the plane is going down, everyone please join me in the first verse of 'Amazing Grace.'"

My girlfriends pulled me back down to my seat and were relieved that no one heard me. The turbulence was terrible when we heard the Captain's voice breaking in. "This is Captain Jonathan, and I'm sorry about the little bit of turbulence that we're experiencing. There's seems to be some bad ice accumulation over the ocean. We should be fine soon."

It wasn't fine. At this point, my friend Sarah began to cry and say "I'll never raise my children."

Another friend said with tears running down her cheeks, "I wonder if I remembered to put the laundry in the dryer."

I took a deep breath and realized something ... *something horrible.* When I left Minnesota, I was so angry and mad at one of my guitar players, and all I could think of right now was, oh, my goodness, I'm going to die in this plane crash and I have been wasting my time harboring anger in my heart. My motivation: *me*! My intentions: *me*! My actions: *for me*!

I began to pray ... "God forgive me. If I live through this, I will go make this right. I forgive the guitar player. Please forgive me. I'm so sorry."

I was suddenly reminded of a Bible verse that said whatever I had stored up in my heart would come out. It certainly had, and there it was in front of me. My one regret ... that I left my home and could be at the end of my journey in this airplane, and I was angry. My heart certainly was muddled and unclean with sin, and I was not ready to die and go to meet my Maker.

Many passengers on the plane were sick, many were crying because of the turbulence. Some, like my pastor, slept through the whole thing. Eventually, we got into the Amsterdam airport and touched down safely.

As people do so often, we got off the airplane, got busy with *the next thing*, and forgot about the thoughts of dying at a young age ... *or so I thought*.

That night, five of us women crowded into a large bedroom. Three of us slept across the huge bed, while two others slept on the floor.

We were all exhausted from the stress of the flight and after while, a strange feeling came over me as if I was being watched. I opened my eyes, sat up in bed and saw through the lights from the outside window, that all four women were sitting up and staring at me.

"What's going on?" I questioned.

"Don't you know?" Sarah asked. "You asked us to join you in prayer. You told us that you needed to pray ... and you started praying."

"What?" I asked in shock (*I hoped I hadn't been praying for a new car or a vacation in Hawaii)*!

Another team member chimed in and said, "You were praying about the naughty guitar player, Bob. You asked God to forgive you for being so unkind and leaving things undone when you came here. You said you were bitter and you felt awful. You forgave him and you were so sorry for how things went when you last spoke with him."

You see I wasn't finished with that whole situation. I thought I was but God knew that I was still in turmoil over the problem. I was still working on that old sinful nature, even in my sleep. Luke 6:45 says that what I store in my heart will eventually come out of my mouth (*asleep or awake!)*.

Ten days later, after I returned to Minnesota, I did resolve the issue with the guitar player because what was in my heart had to come out.

We cannot hide from God, from others, or even from ourselves.

 **Look Up: Luke 6:45b**

"For out of the overflow of his heart his mouth speaks."

The attitude that Jesus is suggesting in Matthew 5:8, *"Blessed are the pure in heart, for they shall see God,"* is not just an attitude of the heart, but first, a daily cleansing of the heart that helps create and perpetuate the attitude. Think of it like open-heart surgery. You have some blockage (*sin*) that's stopping the blood flow (*the Holy Spirit working in you and through you*), and you are rendered inoperable. Now what? Now, you get the blockage removed so that the blood is once again restored and you are healthy, well, and ready to live life, once again. That is, until the next blockage of sin comes in to start the process all over again.

The Greek word for *pure* is *katharós* (*the word pure is used 27 times in the New Testament)*. Fundamentally, it signifies that which is clean, or free from contaminating substance (cf. Danker *et al.*, Greek-English Lexicon of the New Testament, 489).

The attitudes of the human heart tend to be the same in all of us.

 **Our heart looks something like this:**

- **Motivation** ~ Self-indulgence
- **Intent** ~ Self-gratification
- **Actions** ~ Self-centered

 **Look Up: Romans 6:2**

"By no means! We died to sin; how can we live in it any longer?" (*NLT*)

One of the best examples in scripture for learning about the attitude of the heart comes from King David in the books of I and II Samuel, and the Psalms.

Before we dig in and learn the story, here are the facts:

 **The Facts:** David is the son of Jesse. He and his family live in

Bethlehem. He's a musician. I like that about him ... he plays the harp and scripture describes him as very attractive. I'm thinking James Stewart or Gregory Peck. Who were you thinking of from this era?

The story begins in I Samuel 16 where we see that Samuel, a prophet for the Lord, needs to find a different King. The Lord says to him, "*I am sending you to Jesse of Bethlehem as I have chosen one of his sons to be king.*" We must remember this young boy, David, along with Abraham, Isaac, King Solomon, and Jesse from Bethlehem, are all part of the lineage of Jesus Christ.

 **Look Up: I Samuel 16:7, 8, 10, 12**

7 "*But the Lord said to Samuel, 'Do not consider his appearance or his height, for I have rejected him. The Lord does not look at the things man looks at. Man looks at the outward appearance, but the Lord looks at the heart.'*"

And there it is, everything you secretly wanted to know, but were afraid it couldn't possibly be true. God isn't looking to see if we have gray roots or added a few extra pounds over Thanksgiving. He's not checking out our nose to see if it's too long or if our ears stick out too far. The outward appearance doesn't matter to Him. He created us and already knows all about our outer shell. Scripture tells us ... ***The Lord looks at the heart***. So if God is looking at our heart, shouldn't it be important for us to be looking at it ourselves?

8 "*Then Jesse called Abinadab and had him pass in front of Samuel. But Samuel said, 'The Lord has not chosen this one either.'*"

10 "*Jesse had seven of his sons pass before Samuel, but Samuel said to him, 'The Lord has not chosen these.' So he asked Jesse, 'Are these all the sons you have?' 'There is still the youngest,' Jesse answered, 'but he*

is tending the sheep.'"

12 *"So he sent and had him brought in. He was ruddy, with a fine appearance and handsome features. Then the Lord said, 'Rise and anoint him; he is the one.'"*

He's the guy. He's the one to become king. Eventually, David is thirty years old when he begins that forty-year reign as king over Israel.

In the next chapter, David goes on to slay the giant Goliath, and God is with him. David does a lot of running and hiding from a jealous-crazed King Saul, suffers through a lot of battling, and demonstrates a lot of good God-following behavior.

But something bad happens.

 **Look Up: II Samuel 11:2-4**

"One evening David got up from his bed and walked around on the roof of the palace. From the roof he saw a woman bathing. The woman was very beautiful, and David sent someone to find out about her. The man said, 'Isn't this Bathsheba, the daughter of Eliam and the wife of Uriah the Hittite?' Then David sent messengers to get her. She came to him, and he slept with her. The woman conceived and sent word to David saying, 'I am pregnant.'"

 **Look Up: II Samuel 11:14-15**

"In the morning David wrote a letter to Joab and sent it with Uriah. In it he wrote, 'Put Uriah in the front line where the fighting is fiercest. Then withdraw from him so he will be struck down and die.'"

This is the condition of the human heart. It is where sin abides.

The facts: David wants what David wants. He takes it. Bathsheba becomes pregnant, David plots to kill Bathsheba's spouse by sending him out into the battlefield, and the spouse dies. David gets what he wants. God is unhappy. Bathsheba and David's baby dies, and David is overtaken with grief.

Sin separates us from God and produces negative side effects, many times resulting in tough consequences.

It's life. It's our lives. It's yours, mine, ours. We sin. We hide things. We hold wrongdoings in our hearts. They live there and we live with the pain and guilt of what we've done. Blockage occurs from the regular flow of life through our veins.

The effects of a sinful heart aren't just confined to our own lives, but they affect others as well. Sin separates us from God and produces negative effects, many times resulting in tough consequences. For King David, the loss of his child was overwhelming, as was the guilt of his sins.

 **Look Up: Psalm 51:1-2**

"Have mercy on me, O God, according to your unfailing love; according to your great compassion blot out my transgressions. Wash away all my iniquity and cleanse me from my sin."

David is begging God for mercy and forgiveness. He takes it a step further.

 **Look Up: Psalm 51:10**

"Create in me a pure heart; O God, and renew a steadfast spirit within me" (NIV).

In many other Bible translations, the word *steadfast* or *pure* is replaced with the word *right*. David's prayer to God is for help to renew (*begin something again*) a right (*morally and appropriately*) spirit, and develop a heart that longs to please God and live without selfish sin.

God forgives. He sent His Son, Jesus, to die on a cross for us, and He forgives. What does a pure heart look like? It is a heart where motivations, intentions, and actions, are upright and Christ-like.

Rev. Dr. Myrlene Hamilton Hess states, *"It's not good behavior that creates a pure heart. But a pure heart will show itself in how we act. Our motives and our intentions will become clear as we live a life full of excuses, or full of conviction and purpose."*

Maybe today you are asking yourself how could you hear from God and be convicted that your heart is impure. You wonder how He could possibly convict you of something you've done wrong. How can we work at having the attitude of a pure heart, because our tendency is to have sinful blockage.

 **Look Up: Proverbs 4:20-23**

"Dear friend, listen well to my words: tune your ears to my voice. Keep my message in plain view at all times. Concentrate! Learn it by heart! Those who discover these words live really live; body and soul, they're bursting with health. Keep vigilant watch over your heart; that's where life starts" (MSG).

Someone once asked Joan of Arc why God spoke only to her. I love her response. She said, *"Sir, you are wrong, God speaks to everyone. I just listen."*

Developing an attitude of purity within your heart is a natural response to a loving, forgiving God. We listen to Him. We listen for Him. When Jesus is standing up on that mountain, the sun is shining down on His shoulders as He looks out at the crowd, and He tells them that they are blessed when they have a pure heart before God. They are blessed when they confess their sins and accept Jesus as their Savior.

What is the blessing? They will see God. They will embrace the kingdom. They have fought off their sinful motivations of self-indulgence, their sinful intents of self-gratification, and their sinful actions that are self-centered, and they are blessed.

Author Elisabeth Elliot states, "*But the question to precede all others, which finally determines the course of our lives, is 'What do I really want? Was it to love what God commands, in the words of the collect, and to desire what He promises? Did I want what I wanted, or did I want what He wanted, no matter what it might cost?'*"

Developing this attitude goes completely against the grain of every fiber in our being. Our nature is sinful. If we work at this attitude, by seeking God and confessing our sins, our hearts will remain pure.

If we watch, think, and listen to everything that is coming out of our hearts, mouths, and attitudes, we can catch any impurities, and quickly cast off sin. Like King David, I continually ask God to create in me ... *a pure heart.*

 **Look Up: Proverbs 8:34-35**

"*Blessed the man, blessed the woman, who listens to Me, awake and ready for Me each morning, alert and responsive as I start my day's work. When you find Me, you find life, real life*" (MSG).

Here are some steps that will help you to remain pure and upright with God and others.

 **STEP ONE:** ***Be. God-motivated***

Psalm 119:11, "Thy Word have I hid in my heart, that I might not sin against God."

Matthew 11:28-30, "Come to me, all you who are weary and burdened, and I will give you rest. Take my yoke upon you and learn from me, for I am gentle and humble in heart, and you will find rest for your souls. For my yoke is easy and my burden is light."

II Chronicles 16:9, "For the eyes of the Lord move to and fro throughout the earth that He may strongly support those whose heart is completely His."

STEP TWO: ***Be. remorseful*** **of your sins**

Psalm 51:10, "Create in me a clean heart, O God, and renew a right spirit within me."

Psalm 51:9-11, "Hide your face from my sins and blot out all my iniquity. Create in me a pure heart, O God, and renew a steadfast spirit within me. Do not cast me from your presence or take your Holy Spirit from me" *(NIV).*

I John 1:9, "If we confess our sins, He is faithful and just to forgive us our sins and cleanse us from all unrighteousness."

STEP THREE: ***Be. acceptant*** **of God's forgiveness and move on**

II Timothy 2:22, "Flee the evil desires of youth and pursue righteousness, faith, love and peace, along with those who call on the Lord out of a pure heart."

Proverbs 28:13, "He that covereth his sins shall not prosper: but whoso confesseth and forsaketh them shall have mercy."

Psalm 32:5, "I acknowledged my sin unto thee, and mine iniquity have I not hid. I said, I will confess my transgressions unto the Lord; and thou forgavest the iniquity of my sin. Selah."

STEP FOUR: ***Be. selfless*** **and repeat steps as necessary**

Psalm 24:3-5, "Who may ascend the mountain of the Lord? Who may stand in his holy place? Those who have clean hands and a pure heart, who do not put their trust in an idol or swear by a false god. They will receive blessing from the Lord and vindication from God their Savior."

Philippians 1:9-11, "And this is my prayer: that your love may abound more and more in knowledge and depth of insight, so that you may be able to discern what is best and may be pure and blameless for the day of Christ, filled with the fruit of righteousness that comes through Jesus Christ-to the glory and praise of God."

I Timothy 1:5, "The goal of this command is love, which comes from a pure heart and a good conscience and a sincere faith."

Blessed are those who are humble and see what they've done wrong. Blessed are those who ask God to remove their sin and create a clean slate. Blessed is the one who truthfully reviews his/her motivations, and sees when it's impure. Blessed are we when the heart speaks through the mouth, even if we're praying in our sleep.

Questions:

1. Do you currently have an issue of unforgiveness in your heart? Were you fully aware of this, or is it quietly coming out in what you say and do?

2. Are you regularly meeting with God and confessing your sins? Are you ignoring anything in your heart today?

3. Do you have a hard time forgiving yourself? Is there someone in your life today that won't forgive you?

4. How does it feel when someone honestly says "I forgive you" and means it? How do you feel when you truly forgive someone for something they did against you?

Look Up:

1. **Proverbs 16:2**
2. **Philippians 2:14-16**
3. **James 3:17**
4. **I John 3:2-3**

Songs:

Hymn - "*Great Is Thy Faithfulness*"

Contemporary - "*You Are My King*" *(Billy James Foote)*

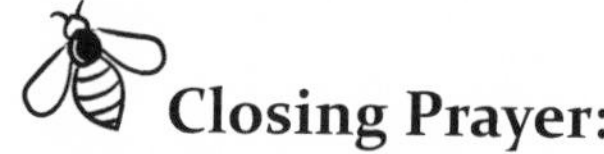

Closing Prayer:

Dear Jesus, thank you
for loving us and forgiving us.

There are many times I am prideful;
often I am harsh
with my treatment of others.

I justify my behavior,
and turn from You.

Forgive me Lord,
help me to be loving and forgiving
like You are to all of us.

Give me a heart like Yours,
pure, clean, and with good motives.
In Jesus' Name, *Amen.*

CHAPTER 7

Peacemakers

"I have long believed that the way to know a spiritual sense is to know it in our real life. I think the best way to understand about God and peace is to know about peace in our everyday lives."

Fred Rogers

Be. Reconciled   Be. Grace-Filled   Be. Blessed

The Buzz: Last week we learned that God's desire for us is to have a pure heart that is free of selfish attitudes.

Matthew 5:9 *"Blessed are the peacemakers, for they will be called sons of God."*

The band filed in one at a time, the guitar player, the bass player and my drummer, Steve. As the men chatted about some recent football fiasco, they took their instruments up to the stage.

I looked back to see several of the vocalists coming in, when I noticed something was overtly wrong. Sandi and Jen, who were always happy and outgoing, walked down separate sides of the sanctuary and looked away from the rest of the team and me. I thought ... oh, oh, ... *trouble*.

As the team chatted and I opened in a word of prayer, I noticed that the normal bubbly personalities of the two friends were inexplicably replaced with a sullen silence that swept over their souls, and was now starting to cover the rest of us like a big wet blanket.

The band headed to their spots, while the others grabbed their microphones and got ready to sing. Sandi purposely placed herself on the opposite end across from Jen, and I was suddenly thrust back in time to junior high. It seemed like something that would have happened in seventh grade, not in the land of grown-ups.

Twenty-five minutes later, I asked Jen if she could take the lead on one of our songs. She mumbled "sure" and everything blew up.

Sandi shouted, "Why does she always get to sing solo spots? You favor her and you ignore all of us! What's wrong with the rest of us?"

"Wow!" the bass player said, "What's going on with you tonight?" he directed his question towards an irate Sandi.

At that moment, it all came rolling out, as Jen faced Sandi and retorted, "Look who's talking! You are continually getting the lead in our special music, you were in a drama two weeks ago, and now you are leaving for Hawaii with your perfect husband and 2.5 perfect children. What's wrong with the rest of *us*?" she shrieked.

"Okay, let's take a five minute break," I said. "Sandi and Jen, let's head up to my office."

They walked separately from me and each other, like they were five years old. I opened my office door for them, pulled Diet Cokes from my mini fridge, and sat down on the couch next to Jen, while Sandi took my chair.

"Does someone want to start?" I asked. What seemed like many moments passed, as silence continued to permeate the room. I remembered how my mother used to break some of the tension of fights with my siblings with something silly and I began with, "My mother just called and said you guys have to shake hands and make up."

For whatever reason, it worked and Jen began to laugh. That broke the silence in Sandi and they began to talk.

Jen told us how her husband had just lost his job, how she had been working extra hours so the family could take a small vacation to a nearby cabin, and now they wouldn't get to go because of the job loss. She felt jealous and mad. She was angry with everyone, not just her best friend. Mostly importantly, she told how incredibly alone she felt and how sorry she was for being so angry.

I talked through the situation with the two of them, slowly and steadily. Together, we made sure that they were both heard, and they embraced and cried, as Sandi committed to help Jen's family in every way she could.

When we got back to the rehearsal, the band joked and teased to lighten the spirit and we moved through the rehearsal without any more conflict.

An interesting thing took place after that night as I watched those two friends bond through a crisis. I also watched them as they progressed to think, talk, and walk through conflict with each other and help others to do the same. They were living the life of true peacemakers.

As Jesus is teaching about this attitude of the heart, we begin by looking at the Biblical background of the meaning of the word *peace*. The concept comes from the Arabic word *salaam* or the Hebrew word *shalom*. The noun *shalom* means "*safe, well, happy ... blessed*."

William Barclay's *Daily Study Bible Series* gives this understanding of *shalom*: "In Hebrew *peace* is never only a negative state; it never means only the absence of trouble; in Hebrew *peace* always means "*everything which makes for a man's highest good.*" In the east when one man says to another, *salaam*—which is the same word—he does not mean that he wishes for the other man only the absence of evil things; he wishes for him the presence of all good things. In the Bible peace means not only freedom from all trouble; it means enjoyment of all good" (vol. 1, p. 108).

You have done your part to get along with those around you and because you have continually met with God, confessed to God, and loved God, your heart is pure and right before others, and so you have a peace that flows from your heart for others.

The peace that the word *shalom* expresses is a deep peace, a satisfying feeling in the soul that everything is right with the world, with your neighbors, with your best friends, with God. You have done your part to get along with those around you and because you have continually met with God, confessed to God, and loved God, your heart is pure and right before others, and so you have a peace that flows from your heart for others.

 **Look Up: Colossians 4:5-6**

"Be wise in the way you act toward outsiders; make the most of every opportunity. Let your conversation be always full of grace, seasoned with salt, so that you may know how to answer everyone."

How do you approach those who are in conflict with you or with others that are in relationship to you? What can we do when people are coming at us with an attitude of anger (*sometimes it has absolutely nothing to do with us as this goes back to be.attitude #3 ... meek and self-controlled)*?

Look Up: Romans 14:19

"Therefore let us pursue the things which make for peace and the things by which one may edify another."

The job of a peacemaker is to reconcile ourselves to God, reconcile others to God, and reconcile those who are in conflict against one another. Jesus gives us amazing examples of how to respond to people with attitudes that are less than Godly. This beatitude, *peacemaker*, pushes us past *how to be* and into a response of *what to do.* Jesus exemplifies the attitude of peace when He dealt with the Pharisees and the woman caught in adultery.

Look Up: John 8:1-11

1 *" ... but Jesus went to the Mount of Olives.*

2 *At dawn he appeared again in the temple courts, where all the people*
gathered around him, and he sat down to teach them. 3 *The teachers*
of the law and the Pharisees brought in a woman caught in adultery.
They made her stand before the group 4 *and said to Jesus, 'Teacher,*
this woman was caught in the act of adultery. 5 *In the Law Moses*
commanded us to stone such women. Now what do you say?' 6 *They*
were using this question as a trap, in order to have a basis for accusing
him.

But Jesus bent down and started to write on the ground with his finger.
7 *When they kept on questioning him, he straightened up and said to*
them, 'Let any one of you who is without sin be the first to throw a
stone at her.' 8 *Again he stooped down and wrote on the ground.*

9 At this, those who heard began to go away one at a time, the older ones first, until only Jesus was left, with the woman still standing there.
10 Jesus straightened up and asked her, 'Woman, where are they? Has no one condemned you?'

11 'No one, sir,' she said.

'Then neither do I condemn you,' Jesus declared. 'Go now and leave your life of sin.'"

Pastor, theologian, and author, Dietrich Bonhoeffer, states, "*The followers of Jesus have been called to peace. When he called them they found their peace, for he is their peace. But now they are told that they must not only have peace but make it. And to that end they renounce all violence and tumult.*"

Look Up: Isaiah 9:6

Isaiah prophesied about Jesus: "*For unto us a Child is born, unto us a Son is given; and the government will be upon His shoulder. And His name will be called Wonderful, Counselor, Mighty God, Everlasting Father, Prince of Peace.*"

Isaiah has prophesied that there will be a Messiah coming who will be a peacemaker ... a Prince of Peace. In the book of Romans, Paul is talking about Christ and quotes Isaiah prophecies from the Old Testament.

Look Up: Romans 10:15

"And how shall they preach unless they are sent? As it is written: 'How beautiful are the feet of those who preach the gospel of peace, who bring glad tidings of good things!'"

When we are living with the attitudes that Jesus teaches in Matthew 5, everything up until now continues to promote the following: be humble, be mournful, be meek, be hungry for God, be merciful, and be pure in heart. Those attitudes start with us working on who we are and getting straight with God. Out of that humility and those heart attitudes, comes that love for one another to help foster peace. It's a peace before God, where we don't have to have our own way, a peace before God where we say we want what He wants, and a peace to share with others. Peacemakers love people and they love to get along and be at peace, in a state of shalom ... happy ... *blessed*.

To be a peacemaker, Jesus says that our blessing is to be called sons (*and daughters*) of God. That means that we are related to Him, connected to Him, called His children. What a privilege and honor for a holy God to call us His children.

It's going to take hard work on a moment-by-moment basis, to ward off jealousy, control, competition, and impatience, and become someone who is ruled by the spirit of peace. If it means having God call you His child, I'd say it's worth it!

 **Look Up: Romans 12:16**

"Live in harmony with one another. Do not be proud, but be willing to associate with people of low position ... "

 **Look Up: Romans 12:18**

"If it is possible, as far as it depends on you, live at peace with everyone."

Here are some steps that will encourage you to become a peacemaker.

 **STEP ONE: *Be. reconciled* to getting along with others**

Ephesians 4:26, "Be angry and sin not, let not the sun go

down upon your wrath."

James 3:18, "Peacemakers who sow in peace raise a harvest of righteousness."

Psalm 32:8, "The Lord says, 'I will guide you along the best pathway for your life. I will advise you and watch over you'" *(NLT)*.

STEP TWO: *Demonstrate patience* to those around you

Proverbs 16:32, "Better a patient person than a warrior, one with self-control than one who takes a city."

Proverbs 15:1, "A soft answer turns away wrath, but a harsh word stirs up anger."

James 1:19-20, "My dear brothers and sisters, take note of this: Everyone should be quick to listen, slow to speak and slow to become angry, for the anger of man does not achieve the righteousness of God."

STEP THREE: *Redirect* negative thoughts and gossip, and *refocus* to Godly thoughts

Isaiah 41:13, "For I am the Lord, your God, who takes hold of your right hand and says to you, 'Do not fear; I will help you'" *(NIV)*.

Isaiah 26:3, "You will keep in perfect peace, those whose minds are steadfast, because they trust in You" *(NIV)*.

John 16:33, "I have told you these things, so that in Me you may have peace. In this world you will have trouble. But take heart! I have overcome the world" *(NIV).*

STEP FOUR: *Pray* for one another

I John 4:20, "If someone says, 'I love God,' and hates his brother he is a liar; for he who does not love his brother whom he has seen, how can he love God whom he has not seen?" *(NKJV).*

Psalm 33:11, "But the plans of the Lord stand firm forever, the purposes of his heart through all generations."

Psalm 107:9, "... for He satisfies the thirsty and fills the hungry with good things."

Blessed are we when we have a peace-making attitude of the heart. Blessed are we when we are calm and gentle in the way that we deal with others. Blessed are we when we lovingly try to get along with each other, and help those around us to get along with each other. Blessed are we when we just sit down and work through our issues. Peacemakers ... it's a way *of* life ... it's the way *to* life.

Questions:

1. Are you in conflict with someone right now? Have you taken any steps to try to resolve the trouble?

2. Do you find yourself helping others work through conflict, or do you walk away from the trouble?

3. Can you think of someone today who has been filled with strife that you could encourage towards a more peaceful attitude? How can you work on this yourself?

4. Do you promote conflict by encouraging gossip? When you find yourself gossiping about someone, do you have friends who stop you, or friends who encourage that attitude?

Look Up:

1. **Ephesians 2:14-18**

2. **II Timothy 2:22-23**

3. **James 3:18**

4. **I Peter 2:21-23**

Songs:

Hymn - "*Turn Your Eyes Upon Jesus*"

Contemporary - "*Breathe*" *(Marie Barnette)*

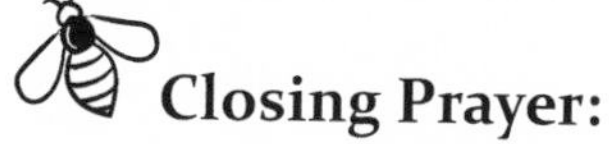

Closing Prayer:

Dear Jesus, help me to be someone
who looks for ways to be peace filled.
Help me to desire peaceful situations
and not search for trouble and drama.

When I am tempted to start trouble,
or to be impatient and annoyed,
give me what I need to have self-control
and be Christ-like.

For friends and neighbors around me,
help me to encourage them to work together,
get along, and invest in one another.
Help me to be a loving person.

In Jesus' Name, *Amen.*

CHAPTER 8

Persecuted For Righteousness

"If you're called to do something, you do it.
Even if you have fear about it, it doesn't matter.
You don't let your fear dictate what you're going to do.
You let God dictate what you're going to do."

Jon Egan

Be. Courageous Be. Faithful Be. Blessed

The Buzz: Last week we learned that we need to pursue peaceful attitudes in how we interact with others.

Matthew 5:10 *"Blessed are those who are persecuted because of righteousness, for theirs is the kingdom of heaven."*

The room was dimly lit, and the night was extremely chilly. One lonely single light bulb hung in front of the room over the pulpit, and I watched it sway a bit as the pastor spoke. I looked around the room. There were only about thirty-five people present and they looked tired and weary, after a long day's work. I pulled my sweater up tightly around my neck and glanced down at my watch. I wasn't trying to be rude; I just didn't understand the language. The pastor was speaking in Polish.

He finished his talk and nodded at me to play the closing song. I chose "Amazing Grace," because I knew that my team could sing the English while the others could sing in their native tongues of Polish, Russian, or German.

When the service was over, the pastor came and sat next to our pastor and team and said we were invited to stay for a small supper. He reminded us that whatever they served us was probably a week's wages for the food, and we should be gentle, kind, and compassionate. Whatever we were going to say or do, we needed to be appreciative.

As we sat down to eat small pieces of bread with caraway seeds, thinly sliced ham, and pieces of bland white cheese, I sipped my hot tea and listened as this dear, old pastor began to speak in his broken English. He was going to tell us one of his stories, and I had a feeling that this one would be different.

He began by telling us that one of the reasons that the room was so dimly lit was because it hadn't been that long ago they had to hide from the police. They still kept low wattage bulbs in the sockets because that's how it had been for so long. We were shocked! "Not that long ago," was what he said and we wondered what he meant.

He launched into his story. Because he was a pastor, he was a target for the police. To not rouse suspicion, he began to learn their names, watch for their cars and try to be polite. Because he was an important leader in his church denomination, the pastor said he and his family met secretly with about twenty different churches to lead worship services.

At the time, Bibles were confiscated and pastors arrested. Every Christian in the small city was starting to meet in underground church meetings. The Christians were bonding, finding strength from their faith, and finding help from each other.

But on one cold winter's night, the pastor answered his door and the police came in and grabbed him. He had been so careful, but he said he was tired out and had his guard down. They burned Bibles and they had confiscated his to add to their bonfire. They marched him into a prison cell. This time felt different.

He told us that he could not understand why, but he felt a little tinge of fear. The police officers were talking amongst themselves, the pastor couldn't catch everything, but heard enough of their conversation and it sounded as though they would be gathering the Bible-convicts up in one foul swoop, and shipping them out to a prison somewhere else.

The pastor feared for his family, for his friends, and for himself. He had made friends with several of the officers and caught the eye of one of them. The officer looked nervously away, and the pastor began to pray.

He went over and over in his mind everything that he had done. Where did he hide his things? Was there money in safe spots for his wife and children, should he be sent to prison for more than a short while? Where were the other pastors?

A group of the men were pushed and shoved and moved into a truck. The familiar faced officer walked up to the pastor's cell and slowly unlocked it. The pastor told him that whatever happened, God was in control.

I remember as he told the story, he shook his head and had to stop several times to keep himself from crying. He continued by telling us what happened next.

As he pushed the pastor towards the door, the officer looked both ways, and said, "You ... you're free to go."

The pastor said he never knew why, but he was spared from traveling with the others that night. The other pastors were released after a short while, but they were trying to scare Christians. They wanted to make it difficult by taking their Bibles, but the pastor said it just made them use their memory banks and remember passages of scripture. When one pastor wouldn't remember a scripture, another would help by reciting it.

Christians became more careful and began to learn signals to warn each other that the police were coming. They'd find safe places to hide their sermons and their Bibles, and they'd have dim lights for Bible study nights, mixing things up by never meeting in the same place twice.

"Those days are gone," he told us, "but you never forget ... you *never* forget."

I looked up at the single light bulb hanging over the pulpit. Somehow, that light seemed to shine more boldly, a bit stronger, and seemed to send a jolt of light right to my heart. How many days of my life have I openly worshiped, proudly recited my scripture, and gladly turned to several different versions of my Bible. I had taken it all for granted. I had no idea what it meant to be afraid to worship God. Yet, I sat across from a man who would never take it for granted again.

Jesus knew all about persecution. He knew about it before the cross, before Pontius Pilate, and before Judas Iscariot's betrayal. He understood what it meant to be refused, ridiculed, rejected, and rebuked. He knew what it was like to have people spitting on you, mocking you, questioning you, and trying to escort you out of town. He was even scorned by His own hometown, and those who had known Him the longest.

Look Up: Mark 6:1-3

"Jesus left there and went to His hometown, accompanied by His disciples. When the Sabbath came, He began to teach in the synagogue, and many who heard Him were amazed. 'Where did this man get these things?' they asked. 'What's this wisdom that has been given Him, that

He even does miracles! Isn't this the carpenter? Isn't this Mary's son and the brother of James, Joseph, Judas and Simon? Aren't his sisters here with us?' And they took offense at Him."

 **Look Up: John 7:5**

"For even His own brothers did not believe in Him."

 **Look Up: Luke 4:28-30**

"All the people in the synagogue were furious when they heard this. They got up, drove Him out of the town, and took Him to the brow of the hill on which the town was built, in order to throw Him down the cliff. But He walked right through the crowd and went on His way."

On and on it goes as we see Jesus and his disciples tormented, jailed, bullied, mocked, abused, and *persecuted* in the scriptures. Jesus isn't talking about people poking fun at you because you were at church meetings three times this week. He isn't referring to the fact that people are whispering behind your back because they see you praying at work. Jesus is talking about the tough stuff in life ... the beatings, the jail time, the harassment, the openly overt sufferings of the life of the believer ... *the brutal murders.* To be *persecuted* means "*to be caused to suffer because of one's belief.*"

Billy Graham says "*Jesus never promised His followers that they would have it easy, or even that they would be in the majority. In fact, as a Christian you will often find yourself in the minority—as you do now.*"

Jesus didn't tell His disciples and the crowd on the mountain that day that

Jesus didn't tell His disciples and the crowd on the mountain that day that you are blessed when you are persecuted; He said you are blessed when you are persecuted for righteousness sake.

you are blessed when you are persecuted; He said you are blessed when you are persecuted for righteousness sake.

Look Up: Romans 3:22-24

"This righteousness from God comes through faith in Jesus Christ to all who believe. There is no difference, for all have sinned and fall short of the glory of God, and are justified freely by his grace through the redemption that came by Christ Jesus."

The enemy doesn't want us to walk freely sharing the Word of God and letting people know that they can have eternal salvation through Jesus Christ. He wants to shut us up and shut us down. He's not interested in playing fair because time is short. It's never ceased to amaze me that with God, we have the *freedom* to choose to believe. With the enemy, he walks around cheating, conniving, stealing, killing, and devouring individuals' *freedom*.

The best trick the enemy can come up with is a continual craze of torturing believers for their faith. We live in a world that is out of control. Drive-by-shootings, school shootings, theater massacres, and thousands of innocent lives are taken each day, because people want to persecute the Christians. Some are killed because of their faith in God, and some are persecuted because people are drawn to evil.

I remember reading the story of Cassie Bernall from the Columbine school shooting. *"A young man in the room that day heard the gunman ask, 'Do you believe in God?'*

"She paused. It was a life-or-death question. 'Yes, I believe in God.'

"'Why?' asked her executioner. But he never gave her the chance to respond. The teenage girl lay dead at his feet."

Mark Moore has written, *"163,000 Christians die every year for their faith. Half of all the Christians who have ever died for their faith did so in this century alone, some 35 million!"*

 **Look Up: II Timothy 3:12-13**

"In fact, everyone who wants to live a godly life in Christ Jesus will be persecuted, while evil men and imposters will go from bad to worse, deceiving and being deceived."

To stand up for our faith in Jesus, means to be bold in sharing about who Jesus is, and what He's doing in our lives. We need to share with others because of His love for us. To think about being persecuted for righteousness can be a scary thought. What if you were the one looking up at the police officer who is taking your friends to some place unknown? What if you were the one looking at the end of the gun barrel answering the question, "Do you believe in God?" How would you respond?

Billy Graham states, *"In the last 100 years, more Christians have probably suffered and died for their faith than at any other time in the history of Christianity. Many of these cases go unreported—but even the reports we do get confirm this fact."*

We stand firm. We stand for God. This attitude of Jesus is one that says, I believe, I have faith, I am a Christ-follower, and I'm proud of it.

Are you willing to take a stand for Jesus in your everyday life? Are you willing to take up the cross and follow Jesus?

Corrie Ten Boom states, *"We must mirror God's love in the midst of a world full of hatred. We are the mirrors of God's love, so we may show Jesus by our lives."*

Here are some steps that will motivate you to live boldly and profess your faith to a world that is desperately in need of a Savior!

 **STEP ONE:** ***Be. faithful,*** **accept Christ as Savior**

Romans 3:10-12, "As it is written, there is no one righteous—not even one. No there is no one who understands, no one who seeks God. All have turned away."

Romans 6:23, "For the wages of sin is death but the gift of God is eternal life through Jesus Christ our Lord."

Romans 5:8, "But God showed His great love for us by sending Christ to die for us while we were still sinners."

Romans 10:9-10, 13, "If you confess with your mouth that Jesus is Lord and believe in your heart that God raised him from the dead, you will be saved. For it is by believing in your heart that you are made right with God, and it is by confessing with your mouth that you are saved ... for everyone who calls on the name of the Lord will be saved" *(NLT).*

STEP TWO: ***Share the good news*** **of Jesus' salvation with others**

Mark 16:15, "... Go ye into all the world and preach the gospel to every creature."

Romans 1:16, "For I am not ashamed of the gospel of Christ: for it is the power of God unto salvation to everyone that believeth; to the Jew first, and also to the Greek."

Matthew 24:14, "And this gospel of the kingdom will be preached in the whole world as a testimony to all nations ..."

STEP THREE: *Be. courageous,* do not be afraid

Hebrews 12:3, "Keep your eyes on Jesus, who both began and finished this race we're in. Study how He did it. Because He never lost sight of where He was headed ~ that exhilarating finish in and with God ~ He could put up with anything along the way ... *Cross ... Shame ... Whatever" (MSG).*

Isaiah 41:13, "For I am the Lord, Your God, who takes hold of your right hand and says to you, 'Do not fear; I will help you'" *(NIV).*

Isaiah 41:10, "So do not fear, for I am with you; I will strengthen you and help you; I will uphold you with my righteous right hand."

Blessed are the ones who love You and are not afraid to tell others about their love for You. Blessed are we when we are persecuted, tormented, ridiculed, and scorned for Your sake. Blessed are we when we're pushed and shoved because we tell others that You died for our sins. Blessed are we when we are afraid for our safety, but You are there to save us, even if that means taking us home to be with You.

Questions:

1. Have you ever prayed to accept Jesus as your Savior? If so, do you remember how you felt when you prayed that prayer?

2. Has there ever been a time when you have professed your faith in Jesus and were ridiculed or mocked?

3. Do you believe that we can make a difference in today's world by sharing the good news of Jesus, or is it a lost cause?

4. What are some ways that you can purposefully reach out to others this week and share your faith?

Look Up:

1. **Matthew 5:44**
2. **Romans 5:2-5**
3. **II Timothy 1:7**
4. **I Peter 4:14-16**

Songs:

Hymn - "*How Great Thou Art*"

Contemporary - "*10,000 Reasons*" *(Matt Redman)*

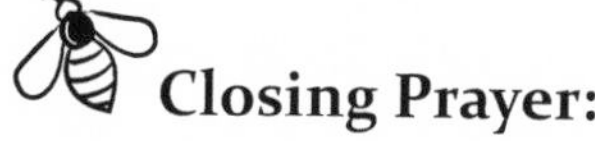

Closing Prayer:

Dear Jesus, Help me to be bold
in my faith in You.
When I want to shut down
and keep quiet about You,
help me to remember
that I might be the only one
who will tell them about You.

I pray today that you will
allow me to share with others
the goodness of who You are,
what You've done, and how
You will become their Savior.
Give me a holy boldness.
In Jesus' Name, *Amen.*

Prayer to Accept Christ as Savior:

Dear Jesus, I admit
that I am a sinner.
I believe You died
on the cross for my sins.

Please forgive me.
Come into my heart
and be my Lord
and Savior.

In Jesus' Name, *Amen.*

Conclusion

Be.Attitudes

*"We choose what attitudes we have right now.
And it's a continuing choice."*

John Maxwell

Be. Focused Be. Encouraged Be. Your Best

The Buzz: Over the past nine weeks, we learned that when we follow the attitudes that Jesus has taught in Matthew 5, we can shape our hearts to live a life that is full and truly blessed.

The Beatitudes: *Implementing Godly attitudes*

I remember the day like it was yesterday. The changing of seasons was close at hand, the trees were starting to take on hues of golds, reds, and browns, while the open window emitted a cool breeze.

The morning had produced a couple of pots of strong black coffee, along with me pacing back and forth leaving a trail in the carpet. I had worried, I had stormed about, I had stomped my feet, and now I was writing what would be my letter of resignation.

Although I desperately wanted it to be so, the fit for me as the worship director at the church was no longer a good one after a new lead pastor had arrived on the scene. I didn't understand why God was allowing what He was allowing, and I have to admit openly ... *I was mad.*

Looking back at all of the chapters of this book, I now understand at a deeper level the attitudes that Jesus wants us to take upon our hearts, minds, and spirits, I get it. I get what I should have done, but in the moment, I only operated out of raw emotion.

I sat down at my computer and began to spew angry, hostile words that would be mailed out to an elder board and a congregation. After being angry along with me, a valuable friend who served as a "*wise counsel*" in my life, gave it the stamp of approval. But something deep inside of my soul said ... *don't do it*. I wanted to, I needed to, I had to send this letter. It honestly and openly expressed the truth about the unfair treatment I had received, and why I felt my resignation would be the only solution. Someone needed to pay for my unhappiness, right?

I felt confused and conflicted, and grabbed yet, another cup of coffee while I dialed the number to a kind friend, who also served as a "wise counsel." I explained the situation and read my soon-to-be-sent letter (*Proverbs 15:22, "Without counsel plans fail, but with many advisors they succeed"*). I'll never forget our conversation ... *not ever*.

He said, "Kathy, I am so sorry this is happening to you. This is painful. This is wrong, but God knew about this before it ever happened, and He is getting you ready for something else, something bigger and something better. Think of it like this ... you're getting promoted."

"You have got to be joking! This doesn't feel like a promotion. This is awful. I have been there, served there, and loved my people. Why do companies hire someone in charge who wants to eliminate their staff and hire their own people?" I asked.

He answered, "It happens all the time, but you already know this ... this is where faith comes into play. You must remain calm, self-controlled, and patient with God. You cannot send that letter. You must take the high road. You have to love these people through this.

You cannot allow the enemy to come in and cause trouble. Don't send that letter. Someday you will look back and regret it, knowing you could have been a better version of yourself," he said.

I hung up the phone that day, tore up the letter, poured the rest of the coffee down the drain, vacuumed the rug and put my hiking boots on to get ready for taking the high road.

What were the beatitudes that day that fit into the scenario? I needed to be humble *(vs. 3)*. I needed to mourn for my sin *(vs. 4)*. I needed to be gentle in spirit, not angry *(vs. 5)*. I needed to seek God for answers, wisdom, and direction *(vs. 6)*. I needed to be merciful to this new leader *(vs. 7)*. I needed to be selfless *(vs. 8)*. And finally, I needed to be a peacemaker *(vs. 9)*. There they were, all wrapped up neatly into one big package ... my attitudes versus the attitudes of God.

As the weeks passed, I learned more about myself from taking the high road. It was lonely, it was difficult, and I was scared. But I found out something wonderful from traveling, I was never alone because God walked with me. When I began that journey, on the path He stood, encouraging me on, telling me it would be okay, and allowing me to not only grieve, but to begin to feel an excitement and anticipation for where I was to go next on my journey.

If I had mailed that letter out, it would have caused trouble at a deep level. Sure it would have given my sinful nature some satisfaction, but it wouldn't have been Godly, and it wouldn't have been the best version of me.

Instead, God began a process of unveiling a bigger plan for my life and a plan for me and my husband to travel on this journey ... together. We purchased an old 1900's church from a rural location twenty miles from our grove, and moved it there for our ministry, Best Life Ministries (www.bestlifeministries.com). Some thought we were crazy to move an old building, others cheered us on, and still others have supported us both prayerfully, emotionally, financially, and physically.

The truth is simply this: I have served God with a great amount of fulfilling ministry than I ever could have, if I was still at that position. God knew that when He called me out of that job. He knew that I had new trails to blaze and new work to accomplish. The ministry is growing and flourishing now, and I look back at that moment in time and am very grateful that someone shook me up enough to say, "Wait! Look at what you're doing? What is your attitude? Is it Godly?"

The beatitudes are filled with Jesus' recommendations for us to live a better life. He wants us to live our very best version of ourselves ... our best life.

The beatitudes are filled with Jesus' recommendations for us to live a better life. He wants us to live our very best version of ourselves ... our best life.

 **Look Up: John 10:10b**

"I came so they can have real and eternal life, more and better life than they ever dreamed of" (MSG).

Walking through life with Godly attitudes is admirable, it's recommended, it's wise, but it's not going to be easy. How can we do this alone? How can we get up each day and face our stressed out boss who is demanding more work from us, or the neighbor who doesn't like it when we park in her spot, or the old friend who is critical and full of gossip, or the sister who requires a lot of patience? How can we control the emotions that we are experiencing that lead us to want to lash out, be impatient, or even worse, respond in ways that are irrevocable?

God gives us help, strength, encouragement, and motivation through His Word, through His Spirit, and throughout our daily journey.

Look Up: Isaiah 58:11

"The Lord will guide you always; he will satisfy your needs in a sun-scorched land and will strengthen your frame. You will be like a well-watered garden, like a spring whose waters never fail" (NIV).

Isaiah 58:11, "I will always show you where to go. I'll give you a full life in the emptiest of places firm muscles, strong bones. You'll be like a well-watered garden, a gurgling spring that never runs dry" (MSG).

We won't be able to walk on the path everyday and be perfect. God did not make us perfect. Only God is perfect. In that place where we are now, and where we will become ... is the *in-between*.

The in-between is the spot in the journey where everything takes place. You have your beginning, where you are getting your boots laced, your jacket zipped, your backpack tied up neatly, and you're ready to take off and hike that path.

At some point, you will have the end of your journey. The path is completed and if you know the Savior, the doors will open up to welcome you into His Kingdom at the end of your life.

What happens in the middle of the journey is that *who we are*, and *who we're going to become* is an everyday process. What happens on the path, each and every day, is how we deal with life around us. How *do* we relate to one another? How *do* we respond to the needs of others? How will we implement the attitudes of Jesus? We will need to be patient with ourselves, and completely and utterly reliant on God for help.

There will be moments on the path when you were less than your best and certainly far from God's best version of who you should be in this life. There will be times when you need to stop on the side of the road, like I did that morning before I sent out that letter, and seek God's wisdom, and seek wise counsel to know which direction to go on the path. There will be times when you will need to just sit down and rest, waiting on God for the next step.

My favorite author, John Ortberg states, " *... waiting is not just something we have to do until we get what we want. Waiting is part of the process of becoming what God wants us to be."*

As Jesus was teaching on that mountain, He looked out at the disciples and the crowd, and He loved them. He loved them for all of their hopelessness, for all of their frustration, for all of their less-than-perfect-version, but He knew they needed a place to start on their journey. That place to start is to implement, incorporate, embrace, instill, and ensure that you are working hard, that you are trying diligently, to follow the path He's set out before you.

This path is a journey of your life, and the beatitudes are the tools that you will pull from your backpack. He's provided this help for you along your way.

Look Up: Matthew 5:3-10

3 *"Blessed are the poor in spirit,*
for theirs is the kingdom of heaven.

4 *Blessed are those who mourn,*

for they will be comforted.

5 *Blessed are the meek,*
for they will inherit the earth.

6 *Blessed are those who hunger and thirst for righteousness,*
for theirs is the kingdom of heaven.

7 *Blessed are the merciful,*
for they will be shown mercy.

8 *Blessed are the pure in heart,*
for they will see God.

9 *Blessed are the peacemakers,*
for they will be called children of God.

10 *Blessed are those who are persecuted because of righteousness,*
for theirs is the kingdom of heaven" (NIV).

When we are humbled before God (*vs.3*), we mourn before Him because of our sins (*vs.4*). As we think about those sins, we are meek or *self-controlled (vs.5)* and in that self-control, we realize we are nothing without the Word of God and a deeper relationship to Him *(vs.6)*. Because we are meeting daily with God, we become merciful and loving to others (*vs.7*). We show mercy, because God continuously gave us mercy and we are reminded of our sin. When we think of His mercy, we confess and continue to remain pure in heart (*vs.8*). When we have pure motivations and actions, we can be a peacemaker in our own lives and in the lives of others (*vs.9*). When we are living these Life-Attitudes, we will be persecuted for following Christ (*vs. 10*). Then ... and only then ... are we affirmed that the lifestyle we are living ... is of God.

These are the tools you have now. This is the map that God has given you, the attitudes to have, and how to *be*, each and every moment of the day as you travel through your life. These are the *attitudes* of Jesus, the *attitudes* of being Christ-like, the *attitudes* of God.

These attitudes are the character traits that you want to be known for on this journey. Jesus wants you to build these into your life, and use them as your roadmap for the journey. These are the tools that you will have to help lead you in the steps to becoming blessed ... content ... happy.

 **Look Up: Psalm 119:5**

"Oh, that my steps might be steady, keeping to the course You set" (MSG).

Dream big ... pray diligently, seek God's will for your life and incorporate these *Be. attitudes*. God has put into every life, a path, a journey that only you can take.

Following His daily directions, you can set out to discover the path He has made for you.

The path means growing, changing, trusting, journeying, experiencing life. What better way to travel this path, then with God traveling by your side, giving you help for each and every step. *We are never alone.*

Look Up: Proverbs 3:5-6

"Trust in the Lord with all your heart, and lean not unto thine own understanding. In all thy ways acknowledge Him, and He shall direct thy paths."

Here are some steps that will encourage you on your journey.

STEP ONE: *Be. in prayer*

I John 5:14-15, "And this is the confidence which we have before Him, that, if we ask anything according to His will, He hears us. And if we know that He hears us in whatever we ask, we know that we have the requests which we have asked from Him."

Philippians 4:6-7, "Be anxious for nothing, but in everything by prayer and supplication with thanksgiving let your requests be made known to God. And the peace of God, which surpasses all comprehension, shall guard your hearts and your minds in Christ Jesus" *(NKJV)*.

I Thessalonians 5:16-18, "Rejoice always, pray continually, give thanks in all circumstances; for this is God's will for you in Christ Jesus."

STEP TWO: *Be. faith-filled*

Matthew 17:20, "He replied, 'Because you have so little faith, I tell you the truth, if you have faith as small as a mustard seed, you can say to this mountain, 'move from here to there' and it will move. Nothing will be impossible for you.'"

Hebrews 11:1, "Now faith is being sure of what we hope for and certain of what we do not see."

II Corinthians 5:7, "We live by faith not sight."

STEP THREE: *Be. obedient to God*

I Samuel 15:22, " ... To obey is better than sacrifice ... "

II John 1:6, "And this is love: that we walk in obedience to his commands. As you have heard from the beginning, his command is that you walk in love."

Job 36:11, "If they hear and serve Him, they shall end their days in prosperity, and their years in pleasures" *(NKJV)*.

Blessed are the ones who follow Your map. Blessed are we when we're on the journey and we use Your attitudes to infuse our actions. Blessed are those who are seeking You, searching for You, and trying to do their best each and every day. Blessed are we when we try to emulate the Savior. Blessed are those who love You, serve You, and worship You. We bless Your Name, Jesus.

Questions:

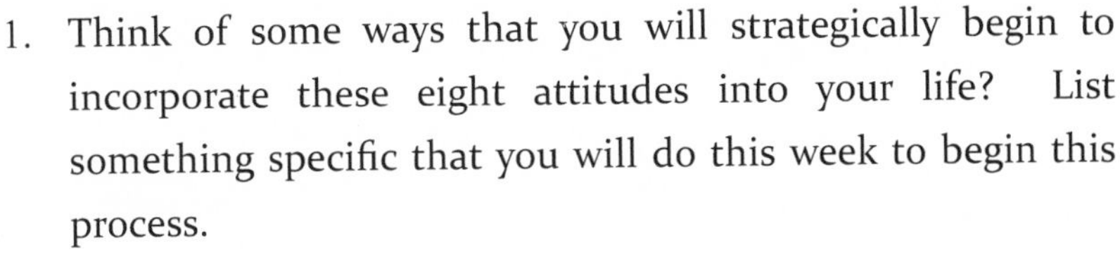

1. Think of some ways that you will strategically begin to incorporate these eight attitudes into your life? List something specific that you will do this week to begin this process.

2. Name one particular attitude that you know you will need to work on more than any other?

3. Think of something that you have done in your past that you need to revisit and repair, or a relationship that needs to be restored? What would be the first step you could take today to change your attitude?

4. List some things that you want to pray about today.

 **Look Up:**

1. **John 4:14**
2. **John 7:38**
3. **Psalm 48:14**
4. **Psalm 73:24**

 Songs:

Hymn - *"All Hail the Power"*

Contemporary - *"Better is One Day" (Matt Redman)*

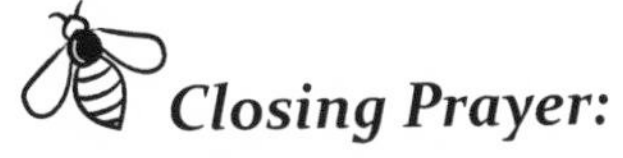

Closing Prayer:

Dear Jesus,

as I travel on this journey
with You, be my guide.

Watch over my heart
and my mouth
and help me to reflect
what it truly means
to be Christ-like.

Please put experiences in my pathway
that will allow me to lead others to You.

Help me to utilize
these attitudes of life found in Matthew 5,
to map out my very best life
and to be the best version of myself.

Thank you for loving me.
In Jesus' Name, *Amen.*

A Note from Kathy:

Let's live

in the moments

that make up who we are right now.

Let's live life working

on *being* Godly.

Let's not live a better life ... ***let's live our best life.***

Resource Page

Chapter 1

1. Temple, Archbishop William. Values.com. 2013 <http://www.values.com/inspirational-quotes/value/27-Humility>.

2. Carson, D. A. contributor. *Expositor's Bible Commentary.* Grand Rapids, MI: Zondervan Publishing, 1984.

3. Marshall, Catherine, Smith-Freeman. *A Woman's Garden of Faith.* Brentwood, TN: Smith-Freeman, a division of Worthy Media, Inc, 2013.

4. *Merriam Webster's Collegiate Dictionary, 11th Edition.* Springfield, MA: Merriam-Webster, Inc., 2009.

5. Freeman, Criswell. *God's Survival Guide: A handbook for crisis times in your life.* Nashville, TN: Elm Hill Books, an imprint of J. Countryman, a division of Thomas Nelson, Inc, 2004.

Chapter 2

1. Ten Boom, Corrie. 2013, <http://www.freewebs.com/strengthingod/inspirationalquotes.htm>.

2. *Merriam Webster's Collegiate Dictionary, 11th Edition.* Springfield, MA: Merriam-Webster, Inc., 2009.

3. Heck, Doug V., Stott, John R.W., Grace Bible Church. 2013 <http://www.grace4u.org/Topical/Beatitudes.htm>.

4. Mahoney, Kevin D. Latdict. 2013 <http://latin-dictionary.net/search/latin/lugeo>.

5. Harvey, Dean H. 2013 <http://christian-quotes.ochristian.com/Atonement-Quotes/page-2.shtml>.

Chapter 3

1. Ten Boom, Corrie. 2013 <http://www.freewebs.com/strengthingod/inspirationalquotes.htm>.

2. *Merriam Webster's Collegiate Dictionary, 11th Edition.* Springfield, MA: Merriam-Webster, Inc., 2009.

3. Maxwell, John. *The Difference Maker.* Nashville, TN: Thomas Nelson Publishers, 2006.

4. Help's Word-studies (© 2011 by Help's Ministries, Inc.).

5. Bridges, Jerry. *The Practice of Godliness.* Colorado Springs, CO: NavPress, 1996.

6. Harvey, Dean H. 2013 <http://christian-quotes.ochristian.com/Meekness-Quotes/>.

Chapter 4

1. Ortberg, John. *The Me I Want to Be: Becoming God's Best Version of You.* Grand Rapids, MI: Zondervan, 2010.

2. *Merriam Webster's Collegiate Dictionary, 11th Edition.* Springfield, MA: Merriam-Webster, Inc., 2009.

3. *Help's Word-studies* © 2011 by Help's Ministries, Inc.

4. Bridges, Jerry. *The Practice of Godliness.* Colorado Springs, CO: NavPress, 1996.

5. Swindoll, Chuck. 2013 <http://www.freewebs.com/strengthingod/inspirationalquotes.htm>.

6. Quote from a sermon published 8/12/1909, delivered by C. H. Spurgeon on 12/14/1873.

7. Mother Teresa. *A Simple Path.* New York, NY: Ballantine Books, 1995.

8. Covey, Stephen R. *The Seven Habits of Highly Effective People.* New York, NY: Free Press, 2004.

Chapter 5

1. Carson, D.A. *Jesus' Sermon on the Mount and His Confrontation with the World.* Grand Rapids, MI: Baker Books, 2004.

2. Barclay, William. *The Gospel of Matthew Volume 1.* Louisville, KY: Saint Andrew Press, 2001.

3. Martin Luther King, Jr., "*I've Been to the Mountaintop*." speech delivered 3 April 1968, Memphis, Tennessee at Stanford University. <http://www.americanrhetoric.com/speeches/mlkivebeentothemountaintop.htm>

4. Ten Boom, Corrie. *Guideposts*, pages unknown. 1972.

5. Kreeft, Peter. *Back to Virtue: Traditional Moral Wisdom for Modern Moral Confusion.* San Francisco, CA.: Ignatius Press, 1992.

Chapter 6

1. Hess, Rev. Dr. Myrlene Hamilton. 2013 <http://www.morningstarchurch.org/sermons/blssedarethepureinheart.html>.

2. Duke, Reverend Kenneth. *Joan of Arc.* 2012 <http://soulsharborag.wordpress.com/2012/04/24/godspeakstoeveryone/>.

3. Elliot, Elisabeth. *Passion and Purity: Learning to Bring Your Love Life Under Christ's Control.* Ada, MI: Baker Publishing Group, 1989.

Chapter 7

1. Rogers, Fred. *The World According to Mister Rogers, Important Things to Remember.* Hyperion: New York, NY 2003.

2. Barclay, William. "The Daily Study Bible: Matthew," Vol. 1, Philadelphia: The Westminster Press, 1975.

Chapter 8

1. Egan, Jon. 2008 <http://www.ccli.com/WorshipCorner/Article>.

2. *Merriam Webster's Collegiate Dictionary, 11th Edition.* Springfield, MA: Merriam-Webster, Inc., 2009.

3. Graham, Billy. *Billy Graham Evangelistic Association.* 2013. <http://www.billygraham.org>.

4. Story taken from *Jesus Freaks* by dc Talk and The Voice of the

Martyrs, page 17.

5. Moore, Mark. 2013. <http://markmoore.org/resources/essays/acts/persecution.pdf>.

6. Graham, Billy. *Billy Graham Evangelistic Association*. 2103. <http://www.billygraham.org>.

7. Freeman-Smith. *Once a Day Everyday ... For a Woman of Grace*. Brentwood, TN: Worthy Media, 2012.

Conclusion

1. Maxwell, John. 2013. <http://searchquotes.com>.

2. Ortberg, John. *Good Reads*. 2013. <http://www.goodreads.com/author/quotes/4215981.John_Ortberg>.